A Wild Estate

twilight years in the African bush

DAVID MUIRHEAD

CATALYST PRESS

For further information, write Catalyst Press at
info@catalystpress.org

In North America, this book is distributed by
Consortium Book Sales & Distribution, a division of Ingram.
Phone: 612/746-2600 | cbsdinfo@ingramcontent.com
www.cbsd.com

In South Africa, Namibia, and Botswana,
this book is distributed by LAPA Publishers.
Phone: 012/401-0700 | lapa@lapa.co.za
www.lapa.co.za

Print ISBN 9781960803603
Ebook ISBN 9781960803689

LCCN 2026942321

Cover photo taken by David Muirhead
Map made by Jemima Muirhead (aged 10)

For my grandchildren,

Jemima, Charlie, and Matty

table of contents

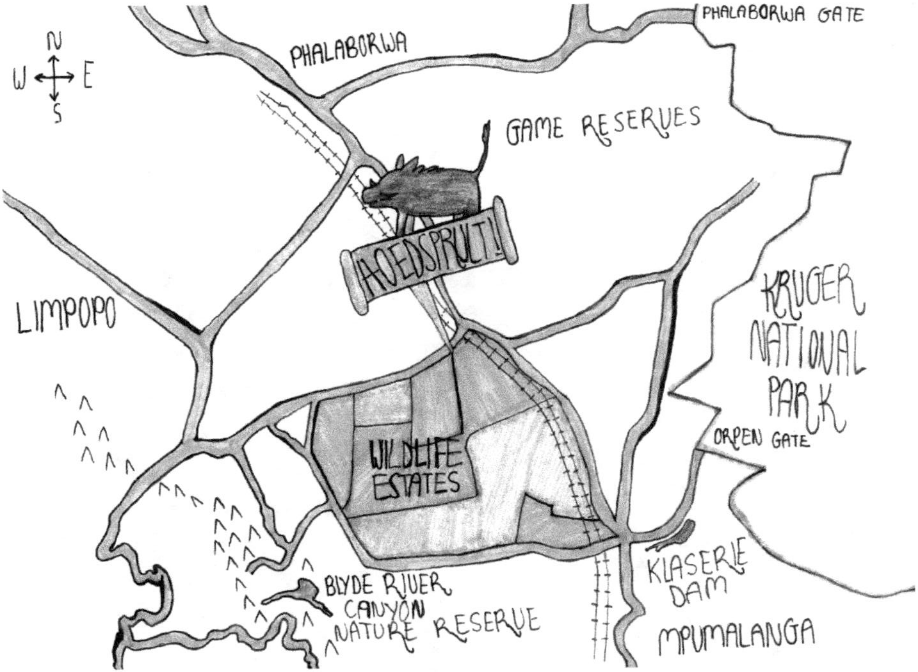
N
W
E
S
PHALABORWA
PHALABORWA GATE
GAME RESERVES
HOEDSPRUIT!
LIMPOPO
KRUGER NATIONAL PARK
ORPEN GATE
WILDLIFE ESTATES
BLYDE RIVER CANYON NATURE RESERVE
KLASERIE DAM
MPUMALANGA

A Wild Estate

twilight years in the African bush

PHOTO GALLERY

HOME IN THE STICKS

COTTAGE INTERIOR

GIRAFFE IN DRIVEWAY

DAVID WITH JEMIMA

CHILDREN &
WILDLIFE
HAVE
RIGHT OF WAY

MARIE & ELEPHANT

MATTY & NYMPHET

K9 CONSERVATION TEAM

GREEN MONSTER

MARCUS

LUNCH AT MOHOLOHOLO

LE BAMBA

IT'S A GORILLA, TAKE MY WORD FOR IT

MAIN STREET, HOEDSPRUIT

ROADSIDE STALL

CAN'T RESIST A COOL DRINK

it's a kind of magic

When you're in your mid-seventies, wild animals aren't afraid of you anymore. Walking along a trail in the African bush, the zebra and wildebeest ignore you or stand and stare in disbelief. It's not difficult to guess what they're thinking: "How on earth has *that* survived?"

Carnivores have a different take. If a lion or a leopard sees you ambling along at sunset, tripping on every second root and stone, it thinks one of two things: "Well matured, age-dried steak," or "No way I want one of those brittle bones stuck in my teeth." In the first case, it eats you, and you don't need to worry about having made adequate provision for your twilight years. In the second, it doesn't, and you do.

Wild animals don't get old, they don't retire. There are no pension plans because nothing usually lives long enough to collect on one. Except elephants. Elephants plod on until their sixth set of teeth wears out. Yes, that's right: we get two sets, they get six. Nature never claims to be fair. On the other hand, we can eat whatever we like, including avocados and, well, elephants. Elephants got saddled with the vegan-only ticket for the cold buffet and must make do with that.

The reason I'm telling you all this is that these wild creatures, and many others not mentioned yet, are now my neighbors. Some of them even share the house. Not the big ones, obviously, though as I write a lioness is lying against the bedroom window on our wooden stoep trying to get some shut-eye. She has two cubs with her and they're playing skipping rope with the garden hose. Or at least one of them wants to. The other refuses to jump.

Wild animals don't make a lot of noise, not like suburban dogs, just the occasional roar, ominous grunt, trumpet, bellow, or chilling whoop. That last one would be the hyenas. The bush is usually a quiet place, interrupted at odd intervals by loud and violent dramas.

On reflection, garden hose is a bit misleading. We only use it to top up the pond. Truth to tell, we have no garden, just the bush, and that's looking desiccated because it's late winter. There's been no rain worth mentioning for the past six months. When we first moved here, full of naive enthusiasm, we planted cacti and other succulents. The elephants and kudus soon got to know about that, and now there are none.

There's no fence around our small house, so warthogs come right up and write graffiti on the walls with their bums. Elephants have done that too sometimes; we've got the gigantic skid marks to prove it.

But most animals keep a respectable distance. There's a certain level of etiquette in the bush. Consider the lioness on the stoep outside. She doesn't bare her formidable teeth at me through the glass sliding doors when I walk past, and I don't go outside and tickle her tummy. There are boundaries, and everyone knows their limitations.

We, that's me and Marie, my wife of forty-five

years, packed up the contents of our flat on the coast and moved to the Lowveld about three years ago at the instigation of our son, who was already living here with his family. "Don't you want to be part of your granddaughter's growing up?" he asked. Roughly translated, at least by a cynic, that means, "We need a babysitter." But for most grandparents, the answer to a question like that is a no brainer.

Our decision to kiss goodbye to manicured lawns and ocean breezes was understandably met with incredulity among some of our aging friends on the coast.

"Don't you realize how hot it gets up there, and what about the wild animals?" one of them asked.

"And you'll be so isolated," another chimed in. "What if one of you has a fall, or a heart attack? Where's the nearest hospital?"

"And what about malaria?" chimed in a third.

"And have you thought about snakes?" demanded a fourth, following up with a long, bloodcurdling story about black mambas, the gist of which was that at least one, possibly an entire family, would inevitably get into the house, curl up behind the cushions on the sofa, and wait.

All good questions, none of which we really knew the answer to back then. Too much worry and exhaustive research and you'll get so befuddled and confused you won't want to get out of bed in the morning. At our age, there's a fair-to-even chance you won't get out of bed in the morning anyway, at least not without the help of two burly men from the coroner's office. So, what's to lose?

As it turned out, our cottage is isolated. It's in a big wildlife estate near Hoedspruit, a small town not far from Kruger National Park. It's a new estate. There aren't many houses and the ones that have been built are very far apart. Our son's house is in the same estate, on a broad, dry riverbed twenty-five minutes' drive away on a dirt road. The nearest hospital is somewhere, over the rainbow, probably.

Hoedspruit is Afrikaans for "hat creek." It was given that name by Dawid Joubert in the 1840s. He lost his hat while crossing a normally dry stream bed, inadvertently choosing the exact moment a sudden flash flood came thundering down. It presumably knocked him off his feet and his hat off his head. He watched his beloved hat being swept away, and was devastated that he couldn't save it. He named his whole farm Hoedspruit, not just the stream, in memory of that drowned hat. Poor old Dawid was killed by a leopard not long after, a terminal event that put his hat loss disaster into sober perspective.

I can empathize with Dawid though. You need your hat up here, to hide your bald patch of course, but mainly to prevent your brain from popping out of your ears. The sun can be vindictive. In the summer months, weather forecasters routinely set the temperature at 40 degrees C (104 F) and the UV Index at "God Help You All."

So, there's good and bad, like everywhere else.

But there's also a strange and visceral magic about the African bush that you simply don't find anywhere else, a deep seated memory in all of us that this is our ancestral home: a waterhole fringed by fever trees where our ancient forebears quenched their thirst, and the fork in a tall leadwood tree, just like that one over there, that's where knuckle-dragging Uncle Grunt ended up as a leopard's lunch. It's all here, all the sights and sounds, and it's all weirdly familial and familiar, even to a tourist from New York.

I can think of much worse ways to die than following in the footsteps of Uncle Grunt, but before that or anything else happens, allow me to tell you more.

tripping

A week before we left Hermanus in the Western Cape for our new life in the Limpopo bush, I bought a new car. New to me, that is. It was already three years old, but the previous owner didn't drive it much, just to the shops and to ferry her kids to and from a nearby school. The mileage was low and, as an extra bonus, she and her husband had obviously had a fanatical interest in keeping the car in a better than pristine state. The brake lights lit up, the indicators winked, and the motor purred with unflappable precision. I felt guilty that we would be taking it away from its pampered existence to the dusty rutted roads of the Lowveld.

Two days before we set off on our long drive north, the aircon packed up. What a heap of junk. What a couple of con artists.

It was mid-February, the hottest month in South Africa. I looked up at the sky and the midday sun glared back, obviously irritated at the prospect of having to keep us company on our long slog of 1,800 kilometers in marshmallow melting heat.

"We don't have that part in stock. We'll have to order it," the garage lady told me. "From France," she added.

France? I pretended not to hear, preferring to think that there were extenuating circumstances to consider, and that she was possibly a maker of miracles. I told her we were leaving the next day, going to live in Hoedspruit.

When I said that, I was sort of expecting she'd shuffle out to the scrap heap in the yard, rummage around for a few seconds, and come back with exactly the right part, No. 8976-Y4524-Z335869-533B16, etc.

"Well, best of luck," she said instead, turning to another customer.

That was it. Whatever happened to a piece of wire, nylon stockings and understated mechanical genius? So much has gone as I've grown old.

"Oh no, what will we do?" Marie asked, when I got home.

We will do what we did when we were young and wrinkle free, and cars had no air-conditioning. We will stick our heads out of the window every now and again and let the air blast the sweat from our brow. Or we will buy a dashboard fan.

Dashboard fans are made in China, so they come in many colors, mostly shades of pink. The three grotesque plastic blades on the one I bought looked like severed tongues. Maybe they'd belonged to people who'd said something bad about the CCP. I plugged it in, turned it on, and braced myself for a big blast. A passing mosquito wouldn't have been inconvenienced by the imperceptible breeze it generated. After a few seconds, the suction cup holding it to the dashboard popped off and the fan, screaming like a Cessna at full throttle, fell into my lap. Yes, not something you want to happen.

Having exhausted our options, we decided to do the

trip in three stages, getting up at four and driving until late morning. By the time the heat became truly malevolent, we'd be tucked up in an air-conditioned wayside lodge.

When you've crossed the Cape coastal mountains, you find yourself in the Great Karoo. To anyone traveling with young children, this is "Are we there yet?" country. It is flat, enormous, and relatively featureless. I-spy-with-my-little-eye peters out after two turns: S for sky and R for road. The answer to "Are we there yet?" is always no. Look at the horizon and imagine twenty horizons beyond that just like it. When you've crossed them all, you still won't be there yet. For the young, the Karoo is endless and boring.

When you're old, that's no longer true, or at least not as true. It is majestic desolation and there are low mountain ranges here and there, rising from the endless plain. I believe this new appreciation has something to do with a sense of self in the cosmos. If you're looking for the center of the universe when you're in your teens and twenties, you simply need to find a mirror. Yes, there it is, and it has acne. One day in life that will change, and you'll understand you're on the outer edge of something incomprehensibly huge, not at the center. And the Karoo, the moody, soul-stretching Great Karoo, is there to remind you of that fact.

When I talk like that, my wife turns on the car radio. She tunes into stations with music being shredded by static. We trundle along through the "land of thirst" as she fiddles with buttons trying to get a station with more interesting static, and eventually settles on one where two people are trying to talk about something in a language neither of us understands. When you're in the middle of the Great Karoo, the radio might as well be tuned to Mars.

But, like everything else, it ends. No one knows where exactly but, eventually, you're not in it anymore. The far horizons are gone and the landscape shrinks, punctuated by hills, villages, towns, and the big Orange and Vaal rivers. Then, suddenly, you're on a six-lane highway in a long procession of 40-ton trucks whose mission is to obscure the road signs, box you in, and force you all the way to the center of Johannesburg.

We don't want to go to the center of Johannesburg. We want to avoid it at all costs. The city is a metropolitan octopus and we're already at the tip of an extended tentacle. If we miss the correct turnoff, we'll be doomed. It has happened before. It is terrible. It is the stuff of nightmares. With twenty kilometers to go, the soothing voice on the GPS tells us to calm down and get a grip. It knows we're old and it guides us onto a slip road to services. There is petrol, toilets, and a shop. There is also a restaurant that serves bargain breakfasts. When you have been up since 4:00 a.m. and have driven through half of eternity on a tight budget, a bargain breakfast assumes great importance.

Fortified, we outwitted the trucks, decided not to argue with the GPS, or each other, and eventually emerged from the urban sprawl on the right motorway heading east. The average healthy seventy-something-plus man can travel 248 kilometers at a speed of 120 kph before his bladder sends signals to his brain declaring an imminent and potentially catastrophic emergency. We made it to Belfast services, and the exit north to Lydenburg, by the skin of my gritted teeth. Never run to the Gents, by the way, it's demeaning, but a fast walk is acceptable.

I remember the road to Dullstroom and Lydenburg in Mpumalanga when it was lovely and lonely and brand new, the tarmac black as night, the center line pristine white. Forty years ago, I could drive this stretch of the journey at an exhilarating 180 kmph, the only car on the road, up and over the undulating landscape, bugs bouncing off the windscreen like gunfire from a Messerschmitt. Nothing I couldn't handle, higher than a kite in my Spitfire, soaring above the clouds, the mighty Merlin engine growling like an angry pride of lions.

"Slow down for heaven's sake."

"Sorry, dear."

The road we were now on, the same road, was a potholed, edge-eaten shadow of its former self. And it was busy. Dodging endless potholes and oncoming cars and trucks that are also dodging potholes concentrates the mind. A disintegrating meteor apparently hit some sections, leaving proper craters rather than mere potholes.

"It can't get worse than this," I confidently predicted.

Of course it can, and it did.

We decided to stay the night in Dullstroom, named for Wolterus Dull who, to the best of my knowledge, never lost his hat in a flash flood, got eaten by a leopard, or had anything noteworthy happen to him. A bit dull by all accounts. But the village is cute, with a folksy frontier vibe. Everyone seemed to be selling pizzas, things called art, and bric-a-brac. You can be sure of good coffee because the Joburg elite come here to fish for trout in the nearby streams and ponds. They won't put up with instant rubbish.

Next day we were back on the road, or what was left of it. I've seen pictures of the Somme battlefield of WWI. Nothing but shell craters, and craters within craters. The road to, through, and beyond Lydenburg had that feel to it. Artillery fire had rained down mercilessly on the R36, and only the R36 apparently. The countryside on either side was untouched. You had to admire their accuracy, but who had they been trying to hit? We were averaging a paltry 50 kph. To add insult to injury, in the distant past, at various points along the route speed bumps had been installed, presumably at the behest of random little old ladies. Remarkably, not one had sustained any damage.

Our poor, poor car. What have we gotten you into? All that pampering and polishing, running little well-behaved kids to and from school, little trips on polished suburban roads to collect the weekly groceries at the mall—and now this? I believe cars have souls and feelings, albeit borrowed from their owners, and ours must have felt what Wilfred Owen felt when he was sent to the trenches in 1915 clutching his poetry book. "One dies of war like any old disease."

Unlike Wilfred, after a brief stop in Ohrigstad, partly to let the shock absorbers cool down and get over their shock and disbelief, we eventually made it through. From the top of the escarpment, the Lowveld spread below, dotted with thorn trees. Or it would have done if the view hadn't been obscured by the billboard-sized back of a monstrous delivery truck. They are delivering much needed supplies to the good folk down below, I constantly reminded myself as we made the descent on the steep and winding Abel Erasmus Pass, grinding between first and second gear in tandem with the truck.

We will soon be among them, also needing toilet paper and sundries.

a home in the sticks

When he was a boy in the 1920s, my father stood on a weighing machine at a funfair. In return for a coin, it spat out a card that gave his weight and, rather superfluously, also told him who he had been in a past life. Turns out he was the Sheriff of Nottingham. He used to laugh when he told the story, but I think he secretly believed it. If the card had said "Maid Marian," he would probably have been less convinced.

You always know who you were and where you've been, but you can never really know who you will become or where you'll end up. You can't say with any certainty where you'll be living forty or fifty years from now, assuming you're still alive by then.

"You'll be in a cottage in the middle of thick bush surrounded by wild animals."

If a fairground fortune teller had told me that when I was in my thirties, I'd have given her a knowing smile, put down a coin and left the tent. What a load of cobblers. I'm a big city man. No, you can't have candy floss, it's bad for your teeth.

Yet here I am standing next to my son, who is now three inches taller than me, and has good teeth, staring at a cottage in the bush. No animals to be seen, apart from two vervet monkeys on the apex of the thatched roof, squabbling about something. Whose turn it is to look for nits in the other one's fur, probably. Vervets have learned how to handle large bipeds, so they're not unduly fussed when we're around. They hang about with the shifty-eyed nonchalance of pickpockets, watching and waiting for an opportunity to grab anything edible.

"What do you think?"

Indeed, what did I think.

"It looks fantastic."

I meant it. Fantastic in the sense of extraordinarily good and attractive, and in the sense of fanciful and remote from reality. I was half expecting the fortune teller with her beads and bangles to open the front door and come out to greet us: "Well, well, if it isn't the Sheriff of Nottingham's son."

Michael designed the cottage and had overseen the building, and some of the builders were still there, attending to this and that. He introduced me to the sun-baked, wizened old foreman, a man I later discovered was twenty years younger than me. They went off together to discuss a technical issue involving the septic tank. Other than the fact that they're temperamental and can send back the stuff you flush if you upset them, I know little about septic tanks. They're best avoided.

Ominously, Marie went into the house with her tape measure, but I stayed outside taking it all in. I looked back down the long dirt driveway. A bulldozer had spent a couple of days carefully pushing its way through the sickle bush and magic guarri and then clearing space for the cottage. Michael had chosen the site for the cottage because there were three big marula trees and an even bigger knob thorn tree. Big trees give precious shade in the hot summer months, precious for us and the animals, so you don't want to mess with them. There is also a view of the distant Klein Drakensberg mountains, better in winter when the trees have lost their leaves.

Seeing as how we're here, and we've got a bit of time, let me tell you something about the magic guarri tree. It's a toothbrush dispenser. Break off a twig, strip off the bark, and start chewing the end. The fibers separate and spread, just like the old toothbrush some of us keep forgetting to chuck out. Better than that, it's a pharmacy. An infusion made from the roots purportedly relieves headaches, pregnancy pain, toothache, constipation, diarrhea, convulsions, and even infertility. Who needs Pfizer? What is magical is that its waxy leaves stay green when other plants and trees shed theirs for the rainless winter months. And finally, if you carry a leafy twig of magic guarri with you, it ensures good luck and keeps witches at bay.

"If you've finished staring at the vegetation, I could do with some help in here," Marie said through an open window. "I need you to hold the end of the tape."

Measuring windows for curtains sounds like a simple chore, but in the hands of an expert, you soon discover how complicated it is. It involves standing on a wobbly ladder and there is lots of pencil dropping and misplacement of notes made on multiple pieces of paper. The height and the drop are not the same, despite what idiots choose to believe. Assisting with curtain measurements, like breaking rocks in a quarry, is work for convicts of the worst sort.

Michael had put in a lot of large windows. Thankfully, we agreed not to put curtains or blinds on most of them. If you're living in the bush, you want to see what's happening outside, what animals are coming and going, even if you're in the bath or on the loo. Granted, you usually have your back to the window when you're on the loo, but when you stand up to flush there could be an elephant right outside attending to its own bowel movements. Who would want to miss that?

The main part of the cottage, comprising the lounge, kitchen, and dining area, reminded me of a modest version of a Viking chieftain's hall, a narrow rectangular room, with big timbers holding up a high thatched roof. Of course there are differences: the chief didn't have any windows, so he didn't need to worry about curtains, and he shared half his hall with cows and sheep. We won't do that.

The centerpiece of the room is a mokoro hanging from the rafters above the kitchen island. A mokoro is a canoe, a hollowed-out tree trunk made by the swamp-dwelling Bayei tribe in Botswana's Okavango delta. Our mokoro has holes in the bottom, so its days of dodging hippos in the swamps are long over. It also has downlights fitted, an accessory that understandably doesn't come standard on delta models.

Michael came back from talking about the septic tank and said he'd show me the solar power system. There were things I needed to know. Fortunately, the main thing I needed to know was that the system would get along just fine if I didn't tinker with it.

"Just ignore it. If anything explodes, turn this switch off," he said.

The cottage isn't connected to the grid, which is maybe just as well given that last remark. There are solar panels on top of the carport, and they've proved enough for the lights, a fridge, fans, a water pump, and even two air conditioners when we need them. The inverters and batteries have their own self-important little room at the end of the scullery. It all looks very high tech in there and the inverters make strange noises, roars of jubilation when the sun shines and a disappointed murmur when it doesn't.

We cook on gas and the two gas geysers fixed to the outside walls supply hot water, including to two outdoor showers. The showers consist of a square concrete base fenced with thick wooden poles. The poles are there to give a sense of security but they're not really fooling anyone. They reach shoulder height and there's a gap at the bottom that would happily admit many things, including a monitor lizard, a hungry python, or the extended paw of a lion or a leopard. I expect the big cats would come over the top in the gung-ho style they're famous for. But none of that has happened, yet. I suppose they're all scared of slipping on the soap or getting shampoo in their eyes. Boy, does that sting.

Maybe that's enough of the guided tour for now. But I would just like to mention the old wooden table we bought from a local farm. It belongs in the room, long and narrow, the kind of table you can imagine Vikings pounding their fists on, beer dripping from their big red beards. Like me, it sags a bit in the middle. If you put a ping pong ball down at one end, it rolls past the center, then back and forth and back and forth until it reaches equilibrium. I showed my granddaughter, Jemima, that neat trick when she was five. She tried it a couple of times, but I don't think she thought it was a particularly big deal.

I think it is. I've rolled back and forth a lot in my life, sat at many tables in many towns and cities, and the ball's stopped here.

essentials

The Hoedspruit I remembered from the 1980s consisted of African women on the roadside selling colorful cloth, fruit, and wood carvings of wild animals. There was more than that, but I'd be hard pressed to describe it. The women, or more probably their granddaughters, were still there forty years later. Carvings of cockerels painted white, with yellow legs and red combs, were popular back in the day, but now tall, impossibly thin, psychedelic giraffes dominate roadside displays.

We'd probably manage without one of those, but before we left Hermanus we'd sold or donated virtually the entire contents of our house. Aside from a few boxes and two pieces of heirloom furniture sent up by truck, all our clothes and other bits and pieces travelled with us in the car.

Marie believes that a car is a kind of reverse version of Thor's drinking horn. Most women do. No matter how much stuff you cram in, there will always be space for more. I'd finally put my foot down when she came out of our empty house in Hermanus with a long narrow box containing a disassembled plastic Christmas tree and its accompanying tinsel and baubles. She'd been saving that till last.

"Don't be ridiculous," I said firmly. "We don't need that piece of crap. The base is broken."

Having laid down the law, I went back into the house

for a final look around.

Magical things happen when your back is turned, but I must admit the tree looked very cheerful and festive for our first Christmas in the bush, if a little wobbly on its makeshift base. I was glad she'd remembered the winking lights.

Like most men I know, and have ever known, I don't enjoy shopping. Let me be more precise, I don't enjoy being an assistant to someone else who's shopping. Walking into a shop by myself and saying, "Yes, that one," and then walking straight out again is fine. If there's a queue to pay, it's not so fine, but still tolerable. It's the decision-making process involved in being an assistant shopper that's so mind melting.

"What do you think of this one?"

"Perfect."

"Don't you think the color will clash with the curtains?"

"No, it's perfect."

"It's a bit loud, don't you think?"

"No, I like it, it's perfect."

"I think we should rather go with the other one."

"Which other one?"

"The one I showed you yesterday in the Crazy Store."

See what I mean?

Shopping for clothes is the worst. Loitering in the women's underwear section while your wife is in a cubicle, presumably having a nap, is embarrassing. I try and hang out in the men's section for a half hour or so, but there's only about six square feet of that. The women's section is a thousand times bigger and it's easy to get lost in there. Anyway, that's the explanation I give when store security taps me on the shoulder.

We were OK for Christmas trees, but having got rid of everything else, we had to buy it all again. We spent the first few days reconnoitering Hoedspruit. Michael had told us about Fat Frank's and Le Bamba, the two shops that apparently satisfied all his nutritional needs. Fat Frank's is a butchery specializing in big steaks and every conceivable type of biltong. Le Bamba is a general grocery store with a hint of delicatessen, particularly known for its large fresh fruit and vegetable section. The two stores are neighbors, abutted by a wine and liquor store, the critical third element to sustain a happy life. There are a couple of chain supermarkets in town, exhaustively stocked and efficiently run, but they're not as fascinating.

Calling a heavy-duty meat shop Fat Frank's was easy to understand (no offense, Frank, wherever you may be), but I was curious to know why Le Bamba had been chosen. "La Bamba" was a song popularized by Richie Valens in 1958, but the phrase's role in cultural history goes back much further than that. In Spanish, the phrase means "the beat" and some scholars claim that it originates from the Bamba tribe of Angola. Many of their forebears were shipped over as slaves to Veracruz in Mexico, bringing with them the haunting rhythms that underscore the song and the dance. I feel a subliminal need to sway and gyrate down the aisles of La (Le) Bamba, plucking exotic items off the shelves and popping them into my basket without checking the price. Perhaps that's what the owner intended.

More urgent than anything else was to get the car aircon fixed. I thought we would have to drive to the nearest big city to restart the process. They would have to order the part from France, and we'd have to trudge back weeks later to get it fitted. In the long meantime we could continue frying eggs on the dashboard. We'd melt like wax mannequins. All that would remain of us by the time the part arrived was sticky piles of soggy clothing on the two front seats. That, and a shopping list and two pairs of sunglasses.

At the back of the back of everything else, hidden away next to a stone chipping plant, is The Boneyard. It has another, more automotive sounding name, but I had to call it that because it was surrounded by the carcasses of innumerable vehicles and their bits. Have you ever noticed how much a rear axle resembles a dinosaur's femur? Some wrecks looked as though they'd been there since the 1950s.

A narrow winding path led through this maze of dead metal to a small office. There was a cat purring on the counter but no sign of human activity. I called out and, after a while, a man appeared from the upraised bonnet of a vintage Landcruiser that had somehow been squeezed into the furthest recess of the dark and gloomy workshop.

It was like watching Jonah emerge from the mouth of a metal whale. He wiped his greasy hands on a greasy cloth and asked if he could help.

I explained the problem and he told me I'd need to leave the car overnight so he could have a proper look. I said I knew which part was faulty and showed him the photo the dealer in Hermanus had taken. He nodded but he didn't say anything. Was I mad to come here? The shiny chrome and glass dealership with all its high-tech equipment had failed. How could this guy, working in the epitome of failed attempts, possibly succeed? Would I end up coming back each day for the next ten years, our gleaming car disintegrating by degrees and gradually merging with the rest of the scrap?

Michael came to pick me up. He was the one who had told me to go there in the first place, so at least I would have someone to shout at when we came back in the morning and nothing had happened, or worse.

"Looks can be deceiving," he said.

Don't feed me platitudes, boy. You may be clever, but only a moron would take a modern automobile to a place like that. I swear there was a Model T Ford at the bottom of that huge pile of rusted junk. Had the owner perhaps come in for an oil change in 1928?

I grumbled and mumbled but I didn't say any of that out loud. I'm only grumpy with my son on special occasions, but I was sure tomorrow morning would be one of them. It never hurts to rehearse.

We were back there early, but obviously not as bright and early as the mechanic I'd been deriding. He must work a twenty-hour shift. Imagine working by moonlight in that shop of horrors with only a cat for company. I thought back to *Christine*, Steven King's spooky novel. Christine is the name of a haunted car, the rusted, broken wreck of a 1958 Plymouth Fury. It slowly fixes itself in Will Darnell's garage over several nights and then sallies forth in the moonlight to flatten Buddy Repperton, the school bully, and everyone else its young new owner doesn't like.

"It's fixed. I re-gassed it this morning."

That was spooky. It turned out there was nothing wrong with the part in the photo. The problem was something else, the ineptitude of the dealer in Hermanus mainly, and it had been easy to fix.

It was like having been diagnosed with terminal cancer by a top doctor, being unnecessarily irradiated by the biggest death ray in the solar system for ten days, and then have the hospital janitor, the guy with the cloths and the mop, casually work out it had been indigestion all along. No, it wasn't like that. He wasn't the janitor in anyone's story, he was a hero, the best of the best. No pristine Italian-tiled workshop floor here, no newfangled electronic gadgets, just practical skill and real experience. It was obvious now the Model T had been a genuine terminal case. And so what if he'd built a hill out of automotive scrap over the past twenty years? We all have our hobbies.

I arrived back at the cottage well-chilled and gave Marie the good news.

"Good, we must get straight back into town."

"I've just been there. What's the emergency?"

"Nothing, but there's a furniture sale on today only, and I want to exchange the shoes I bought yesterday, they're too tight. We can pop into the hardware to get picture hooks, it's right next door to the furniture sale place, and we've run out of lemons."

You can't argue with that.

surviving the fittest

Humans walk or run to keep fit. Wild animals run to escape a predator. A predator runs to catch up with its lunch. The Grim Reaper, the ultimate predator, never walks or runs, or even uses a gym. You can tell how unfit the Reaper is because he's so skeletal, but his hit rate is unsurpassable.

Got to keep fit. I've just finished walking 70,312 miles. The last two miles took about forty minutes. The rest took about seventy-four years. The average man my age, with a similar outlook on exercising, has walked about the same distance. It works out at a bit over two and a half miles a day, probably less than an obese hippopotamus does in a night.

Be that as it may, when you've walked the equivalent of three times round the world, you'd think life, your wife, and the fitness boffins on YouTube would cut you some slack. But Marie has turned on the TV. The familiar beat is playing, and a beguiling female voice has started issuing instructions: hup, two, three (ouch), get your bottom off the couch.

In the middle of the bush surrounded by unpredictable animals, we're not supposed to walk further than a stone's throw from the house, least of all at dawn and in the evening. When we first lived here, we jumped out of our skins when we were outside and heard a noise, bolting for the safety of our burrow like a couple of startled rodents. Maybe a little more dignified than that, but not by much.

We exercised in the cottage or drove out of the reserve for a walk, and we still often do that. A railway line runs down the eastern fence line and we walk beside the track. Freight train drivers sometimes sneak up on us from behind, sounding the horn at the last minute, rattling the fillings in our teeth. You might think it's impossible to sneak up on pedestrians in a freight train, but it happens. The long trains come from big mines in the north and pass through here on their way to Richard's Bay on the coast of KwaZulu-Natal.

We gradually learned that not every grunt in the bush is a hungry leopard. Hunting leopards and lions generally keep their mouths shut anyway. You're not going to hear from them unless they want you to. As our familiarity with our environment grew, we began gauging how relaxed or jittery the antelope seemed, got to know the noises that different animals and birds make, cautiously sniffed the air for threatening aromas, and then walked briskly up and down our long driveway for half an hour in the cool of the morning. If you don't know what a threatening aroma is, try smelling a hyena. You don't have to get close. In fact, the hyena doesn't need to be there, he can leave his smell behind, a kind of olfactory hologram.

I've now done that walk, up and down, up and down, countless times in the past three years, and when I get to the end, I still feel like the last cupcake at a chubby children's birthday party. At the turnaround, the cottage is out of sight and the thick bush is increasingly menacing. An elephant could have tiptoed onto the road behind my back and be standing unseen between me and the cottage, plotting. Elephants can be even stealthier than freight trains. If they sound their horn, best not to be on their intended track, even if it is your own driveway.

I tend to walk much faster on each return trip, eager to confront my fate, whatever it may be. They say only the brave charge towards danger but there are more than a few simpering cowards among them, take my word for that too. The reason cowards run or, in my case, walk briskly towards danger, is that they're not sure which direction the danger is coming from.

Michael doesn't think we should be walking up and down the driveway at all. He points out that neither of us are known for our sprinting skills.

But we don't see lions or leopards, or even hyenas that often, maybe every five or six weeks, leopards less than that, and then not necessarily close to the cottage. We like to think we know they're in the immediate vicinity, though we're often wrong.

A few months ago, I carried my early morning cup of coffee out onto the low wooden deck for a breath of fresh air, glanced to the right, and saw a crouching, notably muscular lioness. She was drinking from the little pond outside our bedroom window, about five meters away, not quite petting distance. She looked up, stared at me, moved her head quizzically from side to side, seemed to shrug and mutter "bag of old bones" under her breath, and went on lapping. I slowly backed away, stepping cautiously because I didn't want to spill my coffee. Have you seen the price of that stuff lately? I also didn't want to trip, fall flat on my back, and spill blood all over the stoep. That would be like sounding the dinner gong.

Sudden movement in the proximity of any wild animal is a bad idea. It's perceived as a threat, which it invariably is for them. Makes sense. If a drunk in a bar suddenly lunges at you, you don't assume he intends flicking fluff from your shoulder.

A month later the same thing happened, but instead of a lion, the biggest leopard I'd ever seen was having a drink. Underwhelmed by my antics, the lioness had taken her own sweet time before ambling off, but the leopard was surprised. He leapt to his feet, weighed his options, which included shredding me, and, thankfully, bounded out of sight. The whole fluid process took him about a nano second.

Imagine being that fit. After incidents like that, we pause our usual morning walks from the cottage, but the pauses don't last long. Out of sight is out of mind and, as Michael has pointed out, we're stupid. Stupidity happily enables you to do a lot of things you shouldn't do.

To our credit, we have joined an aerobics class in town. That's harmless. We got to hear about the classes when I was waiting to pick up Jemima from school.

Jeannie, the mother of another child, told me she was a biokineticist and was running chair aerobics classes at a small retirement village in town. She said I should come along. Up until then I didn't realize how decrepit I must look, preferring a mental self-image of a mature James Bond type of person. Chair aerobics? Where does that fit in? I told her I didn't have a leotard. I didn't add that it was inappropriate for a macho man to do chair aerobics, that I dodged lions and leopards for a living, or at least to continue living, but I did tell Marie about it.

"We're going."

"You can go, I'm not going."

We went, or rather Marie went. We agreed that I might come next time, provided I wasn't going to be the only man. It turned out that Marie was the only woman. The other four were all old men like me, none of them in leotards, apparently. Thus began my initiation into chair aerobics. The classes have grown, and we are now twenty-five, all women, except me. There must be a moral to that ironic little flip-flop story, but I can't think of it. Life dupes you in strange little ways.

I've often wondered whether wild animals exercise to keep fit, or whether they're even fit to start with. Zebras, giraffes, and all the antelopes spend their day shuffling from one bit of vegetation to the next, browsing or grazing. When they're not doing that, they stand or lie in the puddle of shade made by a bush or a tree. You never see them playing tennis. They do pick up the pace when they head off to the nearest waterhole before sunset closing time, but that's it.

Except, of course, when a predator suddenly pounces on one of them. The others in the herd explode in all directions, running, jumping, and leaping at speeds and in ways that spectacularly break and vastly exceed human records for such physical achievement. That's the only reason I've never spent time preparing for the Olympics. You can never really achieve a genuine world record in anything. Name any current record, in any athletic event, and I can raise the hand, hoof, paw, or claw of an animal that would beat it with consummate ease.

The big cats are right up there with the very best in the majestic art of lying about in the shade. They don't move any of those enormous muscles unless they must. They're almost as lazy as domestic cats. But I once watched a tug of war between a team of four body builders, who look like condoms stuffed with walnuts according to one impolite wag, and a single adult lion. The female lion was behind bars, literally. The walnuts wouldn't have been there if that wasn't the case. She held the rope in her teeth, and she won, easily.

It's notable that the tug-of-war wasn't with a male lion, because they're lazier than the females. They're also stronger than the females. Lazy or not, a male lion can drag a dead buffalo weighing close to a ton a long way over rough terrain when it wants to. A bunch of bodybuilders wouldn't pose a problem. And the lion would regard the contest as a waste of snooze time if he wasn't allowed to eat the walnuts afterwards.

Keeping fit, working out, is essentially something only humans do. Dolphins surf the waves, horses prance across meadows, dogs wait at the front door with a lead in their mouth. Everything gets excited, but is animal exuberance truly exercise in the human sense?

Humans have evolved far enough to invent language so that they can brag about their big brains, and we've used our brains to figure out how to break nature's rules. At least we think we have; like all despots, Nature tends to be elastic in respect of obeying her own rules. I doubt she's entirely ruled out flying pigs. Be that as it may, we're smart, we're self-centered and conceited, and that means we want to look good in the mirror, and we want to live way beyond our original design specifications.

That includes me. I've just had a shave and brushed what's left of my hair. Looking good, feeling great, and it's time to collapse on the sofa, open a book, and have a snooze. What? That's what the lions do. When in Rome, that's my motto.

it's Tom Cruise!

I was going to start this chapter with a pearl of wisdom, but I dropped it, and it rolled away. No worries, I can look for it later. It's probably under the couch.

Much more exciting is that Tom Cruise came to stay in Hoedspruit. He was here for a couple of months in 2022, arriving with a crew of 300 and his own private air force. They came to film midair stunts for *Mission Impossible 8* against the blockbuster backdrop of the Blyde River Canyon.

Visiting entertainers have always caused great excitement in small and isolated towns. Marie's Great Uncle Son liked to tell his boyhood tale of a circus troop visiting Molteno, a small town in the Eastern Cape, in 1889. The circus folk pitched their big tent in a field close by and, to advertise their presence, set up a tightrope between the only two double story buildings in town. When the school bell rang, seven-year-old Son and all the other kids ran out as usual but stopped in their tracks, gobsmacked. In front of them, at the end of Main Street, was a long-haired man walking in midair. Not unreasonably, they assumed it must be Jesus.

The god-like status of today's top entertainers tends to illicit the same slack-jawed reaction when they suddenly pop up, or down, where they're least expected. Descending from on-high in his helicopter, Tom Cruise was no exception. Children were excited and women, even those with perfectly good husbands, began gossiping about his comings and goings like star-struck groupies.

Tom stayed at Safari Moon, a luxurious guest house, nothing particularly special from the street, in the Hoedspruit Wildlife Estate. He went to work at the crack of dawn, piloting his own helicopter, returning each evening to clatter down into an open space near the gates to the estate. Burly bodyguards and two black 4x4s waited to ferry him to his digs. Also waiting every day was a small crowd: the women with perfectly good husbands of course, children of all shapes and sizes, street vendors taking time off from hawking their wares, delivery drivers goofing off, three or four grandmothers and, on one occasion, me.

Marie wanted to have her picture taken with Tom Cruise so that she could brag about it to her WhatsApp chums. She'd got a good reaction to a photo of herself cozying up to Roger Federer, the tennis titan, when we were in Hermanus. In the photo, she is beaming and right beside her a relaxed Federer is casually bouncing Lindor chocolates on his tennis racket. He was, alas, a life-size cardboard cutout, but one or two of her friends on WhatsApp needed new bifocals. Their initial reaction to the photo was as delicious as any box of chocolates.

Why I was brought along to the Tom Cruise daily assembly was unclear. Perhaps my mission, should I choose to accept it, was to overpower the burly bodyguards, kidnap Cruise, and hold him steady while Marie worked out the settings on her phone camera. Three course meals have been eaten and enjoyed in scenic spots while that complex process has been going on in the background.

Sadly, a selfie with a flesh-and-blood mega celebrity was not to be. We were still in the tail end of the Covid pandemic, and no one was allowed to get too close. Even those who made his breakfast or turned down the sheets at Safari Moon had to have a weekly Covid test. It was sad because Tom Cruise seemed to be a very friendly and approachable person. A man who works that hard and still manages to wear a big smile at day's end, takes time to say warm words to children and women with perfectly good husbands, has earned the adulation.

For its part, the Blyde River Canyon is also used to posing for the camera. It keeps its clothes on unlike the Grand Canyon, it's gigantic, bare-all desert-bound cousin. Fully clothed in subtropical vegetation, from summits and ridges to the deep blue lake nestled in its bosom, the Blyde River Canyon is a model of photogenic decorum.

It also has the world's second largest tufa waterfall. Yes, tufa, not tofu, I'd never heard of such a thing either. It's a waterfall that flows out of a rock face, as opposed to over the top, depositing calcium and hard minerals faster than it erodes the lip of the rock itself. The Blyde's tufa waterfall flows out of the eye sockets of what looks like a Rushmore-sized gorilla's mournful face. The tourist brochures will tell you it's "the weeping face of nature," but it's a gorilla, take my word for it. Nature is remarkably fond of making mimetoliths, but she's never sentimental.

The Blyde River Canyon is an integral part of the great escarpment, a land of steep slopes, streams and gorges, riotous vegetation, spiders, snakes, army ants, wandering hippos, and an assortment of animals with fangs and claws. If you want to dump a motley collection of celebrities in the jungle to see if they survive, it's perfect. The makers of the Australian, German, and French versions of the TV show *I'm a Celebrity: Get Me Out of Here* obviously concurred.

They finished torturing famous dancers, singers, Olympic athletes, and TV personalities sometime in 2023, so Marie and I drove up towards the canyon, parked the car, and strolled up a well-worn jungle path to count the corpses and inspect the empty set. No dead people but the celebrities' creepy huts were still there on a steep slope above a stream, perched on stilts among sinuous lianas as thick as anacondas. The lianas hung from mighty trees and the whole encampment was encircled by boulders and complicated, prickly undergrowth with a hostile attitude. The huts looked as though they'd been built of sticks by the second little pig, except it was obvious he'd gone over to the dark side prior to commencing construction. Pity the poor wolf that came huffing and puffing.

We didn't linger in case a leftover, half-starved celebrity with wild, bloodshot eyes and a home-made spear suddenly burst out of one of the huts. Instead, we crossed a rickety bridge over the stream and continued up a tortuous jungle path, ending up at a large circular pool of still, dark water. It was the kind of forest spot, replete with waterfall, where you could reasonably expect to find a naked nymphet bathing and, sure enough, there she was.

"Bonzer place," she yelled in a broad Australian accent, rising from the water.

She was a little too beefy and fiftyish to qualify as a nymphet and she had a costume on, which was also mildly disappointing.

"It certainly is," I replied. "You must be from Australia."

"Is it that obvi," she said, in a voice that instantly conjured up wallabies, the Sydney Opera House, boomerangs, and eye-watering house prices.

We were surprised to find a woman on her own in such an isolated spot, but she was equally startled to see Tarzan and Jane's grandparents swing into view on lianas.

"Good on ya managing that path, there's some gnarly bits," she said, or words to that effect.

Wendy, for that was her name, wasn't wrong. We'd shuffled along some slippery stretches clinging to each other like Dorothy and Sophia Petrillo in *The Golden Girls* searching for their front door in a blackout. In case you're wondering, I'm Dorothy in that analogy, the tall one with the deep voice.

Wendy had watched *I'm a Celebrity* and, that, in part, had brought her to this lonely spot, lonely now but recently the focus of so much manufactured drama and excitement for TV watchers around the world. If no further use was found for the huts, they would soon fall apart and recede back into the forest, crumbling lunches for millions of tiny creatures, led by wood borers and termites.

Fame and celebrity are no less ephemeral.

bush school

I know something about bush schools because I attended one myself in the mid-1950s as a wee boy in Mbale, Uganda. I got a prize there for being well-behaved, a copy of *The Little Red Hen*. It's a strange book and it's still around if you care to look for it. Ronald Reagan said it was a tale about the virtues of capitalism, but the communists shot back that the hen was red, duh, and it was about workers reaping the benefits of their labors. I thought it was about a chicken in an apron.

You could see Mount Elgon, an extinct volcano, through the classroom window at that school, an impenetrable forest pushing against the feeble fence at the bottom of the playing field. We were told to stay away from the fence because, despite being impenetrable, the forest was home to a leopard. Leopards eat small children, we were sternly warned, though none had apparently been consumed within living memory.

Southern Cross, the school Jemima attends in Raptors Wildlife Estate, is immersed in typical Lowveld bush and has similar dramas. The playground is peppered with leadwoods, marulas, knob thorns and other noble bush-veld trees, the kind leopards like to hang their bloodied victims in. When a leopard is seen on school grounds, which happens rarely, but every now and then, teachers seal off the area with red and white plastic tape, the stuff workmen put around open manholes to trip up distracted pedestrians. The idea is to keep children out of the area to ensure they don't disturb or interfere with the leopard in any way. I think that's it.

Unlike children at city schools, the kids at Southern Cross are wise in the ways of the wild. Little Mowgli from Kipling's *Jungle Book* would fit right in. Many parents are game rangers, guides, or otherwise involved in eco-tourism and conservation. Those that aren't chose to live here because they have a passion for wildlife and the bush. If a child can't tell the difference between a dung beetle and a peanut beetle by its third birthday, the parents start to panic and consult an entomologist to discuss possible remedial measures.

Bush lore is an important part of the curriculum. On a stroll near the school, it's not unusual to come across a line of young kids dressed in green and khaki dutifully following in the footsteps of a teacher. Every now and again they halt, gather around the sage, and learn something new about a bush, a tree, a leaf, a bird on a branch, tracks in the sand, old poo and new poo. Occasionally, a giraffe joins in from a discreet distance, listening intently and staring down with the curious mix of aloofness and curiosity unique to their species.

If I have given the impression that teachers casually march their charges into harm's way, let me pause and add that there are no lions, elephants, buffalo, or rhinos in Raptors, or in the Hoedspruit Wildlife Estate. These heavy hitters live in our estate or ones like it, far from town. Leopards are the exception, agile enough to come and go as they please regardless of fences and red (and white) tape, but they're nocturnal here so the chance of bumping into one on a daylight walk is vanishingly small. In any event, a leopard will hear, see, or smell you (nothing personal) before you get close, and probably be long gone when you get to where it was.

Standing in for Michael and Georgina at school assembly is something we're very happy to do. They're busy people and they ask us now and again.

I used to hate school assembly when I was a kid, but attending as a grandparent isn't a problem. I get to sit on a chair, for a start, not a bench or cross-legged on the floor. I can nod off during speeches and won't get detention. I can even rummage around in a noisy packet of potato chips, attracting nothing more than jealous or disapproving looks. I don't do that of course, I have manners, I'm old school. Besides, Marie's sitting right next to me with a sharp elbow. But nobody is likely to demand I stand up and be stared at because of a transgression, not like the old days.

Between the beginning and the end, speeches are made, jokes cracked, and awards and certificates handed out, lots of awards and lots of certificates. The audience claps, occasionally cheers, and eventually people start glancing at their watches. And then disaster strikes for some parents and grandparents. It was, is, or is about to be their little wombat's birthday and that means they get pulled to the stage to sing and dance and look ridiculous. The mothers generally do better than the fathers, but they both get a lollipop to compensate for the humiliation.

Assemblies often end with ten or twenty older children sitting in a row, pounding African drums. The sound blasts through the intervening space and reverberates in all the hidden cavities and chambers in your body. You listen with your heart and other internal organs, as much as your ears; the physical sensation is remarkable.

The beat of drums used to be as redolent of Africa as the cry of a fish eagle and the roar of a lion, but it is, alas, a fading art. It's also a fading science. Before the advent of the telegraph and telephone, let alone the internet, it was the main means of long-distance communication in many parts of the continent. Skilled drummers were held in great esteem, occupying high office in royal courts and chiefdoms. They used sophisticated musical tones and notes, employing a variety of drums to send and relay messages as complex as anything that can be sent by WhatsApp these days. And the content was probably more profound: news of the deaths of prominent chiefs, births, marriages, your mother-in-law is coming to visit, outbreaks of disease, and the progress of wars. Thanks to the huge network of drummers, the defeat and death of General Gordon in Khartoum was apparently known widely by Africans across Africa long before it reached Imperial outposts through official British channels, as was the death of Queen Victoria.

The school drummers play because they enjoy it, but the solemn look on their young faces suggests they're aware that the drums they hold between their knees are more than musical instruments. In many African cultures, drums were thought to be able to send messages to the ancestors, requesting rain and other interventions, and who knows whether that worked or not. Maybe the ancestors will do anything for a bit of peace and quiet. As the kids pound away, each boom echoes off the classroom walls, trees, and branches, reaching back into a past that's cloudy but not forgotten.

And then there are plays. Small schools in little towns always seem to be good at putting on theatrical productions. It was like that in Mbale and it's like that here. There aren't as many attractions and sophisticated entertainments as cities provide, so a school play looms large in the social calendar.

There seems to be a pattern. At the center, there's a middle-aged person, usually with a vague and mysterious past in theatre, a love for kids and no kids of their own; she or he becomes the impresario. There is a mum with a previously undiscovered talent for decoration, designing scenery, and finding props. And there's a handyman dad who knows about sound systems, spotlights, and dimmer switches, and how to make a castle and clouds out of cardboard. That there are mothers and grandmothers who know a lot about makeup and wardrobes goes without saying.

The last school production we watched was *Snow White*. We were warned to get there early, and as predicted the school hall was soon packed to capacity, night was falling and there was barely a sneeze. If not a cast of thousands, at least every single child in the junior school got to take part. Selecting seven dwarves wasn't a problem because all the inhabitants of Grade 1 naturally looked up to the Grade 4 Snow White towering above them. Those that weren't dwarves filled the stage as forest creatures or some colorful form of mobile vegetation. The palace guards looked fierce with their tin foil spears, as fierce as an eight-year-old can look, and the wicked Queen managed to appear wicked and yet heartwarmingly cute.

My main takeaway, apart from the fact that Jemima obviously danced with the grace of an angel, was the mirror, mirror on the wall. A young girl stood on a wobbly stool and spoke through a picture frame hanging from the ceiling. It was much more convincing than some of the CGI versions I've seen in films.

Albert Einstein said, "If you want your child to be intelligent read them fairy tales; if you want them to be more intelligent read them more fairy tales." And if you want them to grow up to solve the riddles of the universe let them dress up and be in a fairy tale, at least for an hour or two, now and then.

the marula massacre

In the normal pursuit of a happy life, it's best to avoid arguing with elephants. We don't speak the same language, and they have a weight advantage, short fuses, and long memories.

Elephants visited us often in the months following our move to the bush. On one occasion, a herd of fifteen, including a toddler and teenagers, spent the whole night clustered around the cottage. It was flattering to be the center of attention but also a little bit scary. We felt as though we were in a doll's house. One big tusker took a particular interest in what was on TV, edging closer and closer until his left eyeball was almost up against the top of the play-play windowpane. He gently tapped the glass a few times with the tip of a tusk, maybe hinting that he'd like to join us on the couch or, more likely, suggesting we change the channel. We turned the TV off and went to bed, hoping he wouldn't rip off the side of the house to look for the remote.

The following morning, they quietly went on their ponderous way, leaving enough deposits to satisfy the aspirations of ten thousand dung beetles. No constipation problems in that herd. They didn't do any real damage to the trees, ripping branches off the sickle bushes but largely leaving the marula trees alone. Sickle bushes are bossy plants and like to take over, a bit like John Wyndham's triffids, waving their thorny branches around in the wind and shredding leaves and buds from their respectable neighbors. Having plants like that put firmly in their place is a good thing.

Early one morning, a week or so after that benign and vaguely spiritual event, a solitary young male elephant appeared. He made straight for the marula closest to the deck and began helping himself to leaves and twigs. Nothing wrong with that, but then he wrapped his trunk around a branch and started tugging. The branch didn't give, so he changed his mind and started pushing against the trunk with his head, rocking the young tree to and fro. That was too much for Marie. She stuck her head out of the window and asked him to kindly cease and desist. No, let me recall it properly, she yelled at the top of her lungs, and she didn't use pompous lawyer language.

"Voetsek," she bellowed two or three times, banging the wall below the window and following up with a string of epithets I'm too delicate to repeat.

The startled young elephant backed up, raised his head, and spread his ears. He let out a strangely garbled trumpet blast, reflecting his confusion, shock, and indignation, and blundered away through the sickle bush with his tail between his legs.

"I think you upset him," I said.

"He upset me. We need the shade."

That was true. The tree's canopy spread out over our low deck and blocked the hot afternoon summer sun from streaming into the cottage. We often sat in its shade and watched the birds, while a semi-resident squirrel kept a beady eye on us. The squirrel was a bit of a nuisance sometimes, darting into the house if we'd left the sliding doors open to help himself to snacks on the table.

While we were congratulating ourselves on saving the tree, the young elephant had obviously scuttled off in search of his dad. He came back in mid-afternoon, swaggering into view with two huge bulls in tow. Either one of them could have been his dad, who knows, but neither of them looked like the types who would take kindly to being told to voetsek by a little old lady, or anybody else who weighed less than a bus.

I could see Marie was warming up for round two, pumping her small fists and listening for the bell, so I suggested she cool it. We waited, watching through the lounge sliding doors. The big bulls didn't take any notice of us, and it was soon obvious they were here for the marulas, not to avenge junior. To prove it, one of them bounced him out of the way with a swing of his enormous hips to get into a better position to tackle the tree. Junior staggered sideways and collided with a wall of the cottage. The sour bespectacled face of an insurance assessor immediately popped up in my mind, but it turned out there were no cracks, just a jumbo-sized smudge which I thought would wash off but never has.

The first big branch to fall landed with an almighty thump on the deck, landing two feet short of smashing the glass sliding doors. To his credit the big bull immediately pulled it back off the planks, not to be tidy but to get at the new growth on the tip. Elephants won't step onto the deck because they know it will give way under their weight. I've watched one or two tentatively try it out and decide that.

Behind all this commotion, the biggest bull was systematically wrecking the biggest marula. He didn't try and push it over, preferring to demolish it bit by bit. To snap the biggest branches, some thicker than telephone poles, he stood on his hind legs like a circus elephant, wrapped his trunk around a branch and used his weight to crack it and bring it down. The dense crown of one big branch fell into our small plunge pool at the end of the deck.

The mayhem went on for nearly an hour and the three of them continued feeding off the fallen branches well into the night. Lying in bed, listening to Marie's soft snores and the irritating cracking, crunching, and munching sounds coming from outside, I had a rethink. I considered prodding her so she'd wake up angry and storm outside to tell the elephants to voetsek. Nah, too late for that. Instead, I nodded off and dreamed of very fat men messily feasting on giant lobsters.

In the morning, they were gone, and so were the trees. Three jagged stumps remained. They were surrounded by a jumble of fallen branches, some too heavy for us to move. They would have to be sawed into more manageable sections. The pool looked like a mangrove swamp, but the falling branch hadn't caused any structural damage as far as I could see. Despite taking a direct hit, the deck had also remained relatively unscathed, but it was covered in a carpet of leaves and twigs, so it was difficult to be sure. Beetles, ants, and spiders were scuttling about in profusion and confusion. One minute they'd been living the high life and suddenly everything came crashing down.

The squirrel had presumably found alternative digs. As I was thinking that thought, I spotted him high on a branch of the African wattle tree on the far side of ground zero, warming himself in the early morning sun. The small creatures of the bushveld don't fret about disasters; they get on with life without a mumble or a grumble. There are no handwringers and whingers. The world is constantly changing around them, so they must make a plan, or die. D.H. Lawrence put it best: "I never saw a wild thing sorry for itself. A small bird will drop frozen dead from a bough without ever having felt sorry for itself."

Well, I felt sorry for myself. It was startling to see the Klein Drakensberg mountains being lit up by the yellow rays of the rising sun. They'd been hidden by the trees all summer, but we now had a clear view. Yes, very nice, but what about this afternoon? That big ball of blazing gas is going to move across the sky and focus nine tenths of its sixty zillion quadrillion megawatts of blistering energy on our little house. No trees to soak that up and give us shade.

In the following weeks, we were constantly told by

visitors with sunny dispositions that the elephants had done us a favor. It's against the reserve rules to fell any indigenous tree that's more than a certain diameter and all three marulas had been way beyond that. But we had never wanted to chop them down, we did our best to keep them up. I had only this to say to those visitors: thanks for coming, hope you enjoyed the tea, now voetsek before I set the squirrel on you.

interlopers

Everybody loves bushbabies. It's all in the name. So how come there's a family of the little bastards up there in the thatch above our front door that likes throwing rocks at me? Maybe I'm exaggerating, more like little bits of thatch and tiny chips of masonry from time to time. Maybe dislodging, not throwing. But I know they're hiding up there. I see them go out at night, bouncing into the nearest sickle bush like fluffy rubber balls.

If you build a house in the middle of the bush, it's never just for you. It's a habitat for a wide variety of creatures that were already living thereabouts and regard you as the intruder, or at least as a weird creature sharing the huge hollow boulder that's suddenly popped up in their midst. They feel perfectly entitled to make use of the house and all its handy features with never a hint of paying rent.

Bushbabies may be the cutest, but they aren't the only interlopers. Let's go round to the other side and meet the bats. They've found a cozy roost under the eaves, clinging on upside down where the wall meets the thatch. There are three of them now, but I've seen eight lined up like little topsy turvy undertakers waiting for a hearse to arrive. Like the bushbabies, bats also snooze all day and only flap out when the sun slips down behind the mountains.

There are more upsides than downsides in having

squatting bats around. They're fun to watch when they get airborne in the gathering dusk. Their *Top Gun* acrobatics are amazing: they duck and dive and loop the loop, hoovering up mosquitos and other tiny irritating flying bugs by the hundreds and thousands. I raise my glass and cheer them on, especially when a mosquito somehow gets past their sonar system and bites me on the ankle.

The downside is that eating so many insects before daytime means that bats poo a lot. I sweep the deck beneath their roost at regular intervals, hoping they don't poop on me while I'm doing it. Hasn't happened so far and it's a small price to pay for a little mosquito protection. Given time, I might go into the guano business.

Red-headed weavers have also found a home under the eaves. Each year they build a nest hanging from the chicken wire that protects the thatch from baboons and monkeys. Baboons have been known to dig their way through unprotected thatch to get inside and raid the fridge. The whole roof is tightly covered by chicken wire. Sounds ghastly but you barely notice it.

The weavers' nests also happen to hang right outside the window, directly in front of my desk. Come breeding season, the male darts back and forth like a bird possessed with bits of grass and the occasional leaf, only pausing momentarily to sew and stitch. It takes him about three days to produce his masterpiece, and he even goes on to construct a hanging garden of sorts in that time. No lunch hours or tea breaks. Would that the builders of the cottage had been imbued with the same sense of urgency and precision.

The weavers have their own problems with interlopers. Last year, a red-chested cuckoo tried to lay an egg in their nest. I glimpsed her go in as quick as a flash, but it was only when the female weaver also appeared and feathers flew that I realized it must have been a cuckoo. The weaver had presumably been lured from her nest by the calls of the cuckoo's mate. Whether an egg was laid in the seconds before the interloper was booted out, I don't know. No eggs were ejected from the nest that I could see, so probably not.

The weavers' problems weren't over. A bush snake managed to climb up the frame of the aluminum sliding doors, heading for the nest. If I hadn't witnessed the climb, I wouldn't have believed it possible. It managed by plugging itself into the narrow channel between the door and the frame and somehow shunted itself up. A remarkable achievement, but all in vain because it couldn't bridge the gap between the top of the door and the dangling nest. In the end it overreached and fell onto the deck in an ignominious heap.

Another accident-prone bush snake got into the house. It may even have been the same one because it happened not long after the ascent of Mount Aluminum. It curled up under the cushion on one of the dining room chairs and Laira, my niece, sat on it. She was visiting from the UK with her husband Jake and their two boys for a couple of weeks. We'd moved out to give them the use of the cottage and stayed with Michael and Georgie.

Laira sensed something squirmy and quickly leapt up, lifted the cushion and there was the snake, coyly curled up, none the worse for wear and determined to stay put.

Cool as a cucumber, Jake took a photo and sent it through to me with a question: "Something to worry about?"

Bush snakes are not venomous, but Jake didn't know that. He's from the Midlands of England where snakes on chairs, well, never happen. When I told him the snake was harmless, he picked it up like a floppy stick and dropped it outside the kitchen door. It immediately slithered back inside before he could close the door, heading straight to its rightful place at the head of the table. Jake carried it out a second time, dropped it in the grass far from the door, and sprinted back so it couldn't overtake him.

We're wary of snakes. One almost ate baby Michael. Marie was nursing him on the deck at Hoog in die Takke, which literally means "high in the trees" and "drunk as a skunk" in colloquial Afrikaans. It was a holiday house on the coast belonging to her parents. The branch of a candlewood tree hung over a bench on the deck and that's where Marie sat nursing baby Michael. Watching her from a low branch directly overhead was a *boomslang*. To her enduring credit, when she saw the snake, she kept calm and went indoors. Only then did she scream her head off.

First to react was Fat Steve, the neighbor from next door, who burst onto the scene with a can of beer in one hand and a revolver in the other. Alarmed by the commotion, the boomslang slithered up onto the roof and disappeared. The consensus was that it had gone into the attic and Fat Steve, two sheets to the wind and *hoog in die takke*, volunteered to go up through the small trap door in the kitchen ceiling with his revolver and sort it out. The cold reality of a small trap door and a very large Steve firmly intervened. I don't know where the snake went but it didn't bother us again.

Baboons, and to a lesser extent monkeys, are the most notorious interlopers. They don't want to live with you, they just want to steal stuff and trash the place. We haven't had any problem with them. They usually give us a wide birth, maybe because they don't like the glowering, cantankerous look on my face, or maybe because an elephant told them not to mess with the little old lady. Baboons like swimming when it's hot and they've had a pool party now and then when we've been gone for a few days, resulting in a muddy mess and enough fingerprints on the windows to keep the FBI busy for months.

The vervet monkeys are more petite. I could say they're more refined, they'd appreciate that, but it isn't true. They poo on the windowsills and chew the insulation around the air-conditioning pipes. A big male with blue balls strolled in through the sliding doors when I had my head down writing stuff like this, but I saw him on his way to the fruit bowl in the kitchen. I thought it would be out of sight, but they miss nothing. Even when I stood up from the desk, he hesitated before scampering back out of the door. An apple has the same gravitational pull as Jupiter as far as a monkey's concerned.

Leven ende laeten leven, live and let live, wrote Gerard de Malynes in 1622. Through all the wars we've waged before and since, we still say it as though we mean it. It's the same in the bush.

a place for all reasons

In the Ashdown Forest, in the county of East Sussex in England, is a wooden bridge called Pooh Sticks Bridge. It's featured in A.A. Milne's classic children's tale, *Winnie the Pooh*, and it's the place where the gentle game of Poohsticks originated. Best played by the young at heart and the young in fact, the rules of the game are simple: competitors simultaneously drop a stick on the upstream side of the bridge and then rush to the downstream side to argue about whose floats out first. It may not be as cerebral as chess or as arduous as tennis, but it passes the time. It also vaguely hints, as all games strangely do, at the capricious nature of life.

Twigs can get caught in an eddy in a stream, swirling around and around until chance propels them back out again into the main channel and they vanish from view. It's a bit like that with some of the people who choose to live here for a while. They arrive from a mainstream city existence, buy or rent a house, settle in, join groups, send their kids to the local school, and eventually start wondering whose bloody idea was this anyway. Nevertheless, after a year or so, they're recognized by everyone else as locals, as "Hoedies," the epithet applied to members of the tribe.

Apart from time spent, Hoedies have other qualifying characteristics. They affirm by word and deed that they are living in paradise, if not the original Eden, at least a very good facsimile. They react badly to criticism of life in the bushveld, even when the topic is something as mundane and maddening as an incompetent and lazy plumber. Whatever the plumber's faults, which include being worse than no plumber at all, he's been here for years and years and is thus high up in the Hoedie social rankings.

People who utter such outright blasphemies as "No wonder Hell and Hoedspruit both begin with H" soon find themselves cast into the wilderness. They're already in the wilderness of course, that's what they're really complaining about. They mutter and grumble while they wait for a sudden surge in the stream that will expel them from the eddy.

Many people are here to work. Tourism brings with it a host of ancillary business opportunities, gradually at first and then in increasing diversity and numbers. One cafe, then two, then maybe one or two too many. Five waiters then five hundred. Back in the 1970s, a tin shed sold tires and fixed cars that choked or broke on the dusty rutted roads. Now we have gleaming chrome and glass showrooms, forecourts full of state-of-the-art, best-tech game-viewing 4x4s—not to mention a bespoke outfitter on hand to measure each one for canvas awnings and seat covers, to protect passengers from the dust and blazing sun.

One aftermath of the Covid pandemic, here and everywhere else, was that some people who were forced to stay and work at home discovered that home could be anywhere and working at home could be cheaper and more productive than propping up the water cooler in a city office. Small towns like Hoedspruit with a lifestyle to offer have benefitted from this revelation.

Those who live here permanently, whether working, comfortably retired, or rich and idle, live in the town itself or on one of the residential wildlife estates that encircle it. The first relatively high-density residential wildlife estate close to town to be developed was Raptor's View, soon followed by the Hoedspruit Wildlife Estate. These estates were developed and built back then because there was an existing local need for more housing, but also in the hope and expectation that there were people from the rest of the country, and maybe the rest of the world, who would want to live cheek-by-jowl with wild animals, if not forever then at least for a month or two each year. It wasn't strange that a global disease and internet access helped that dream come true.

Oddly, there seems to be an unusual number of foreign, faintly mysterious single women in their forties living hereabouts, not that I've personally conducted a census. Living, not so much working. They seem to have lots of money, and there's often a discarded husband or lover in their recent past, now far away and dismissively mentioned in passing.

When they were young, they probably watched Meryl Streep playing Karen von Blixen in *Out of Africa*, and they've promised themselves the same romantic experience. They buy a house in the bush with an expansive veranda and then languish on a settee, sipping tea or gin depending on the time of day, and wait for a Robert Redford look-alike in shorts, a sweat-stained shirt, and a hat to happen by. He'll have eyes as blue as Africa's skies and will probably be carrying a rifle with a nonchalance that betrays its repeated deadly use. Clearly the kind of man who won't swoon in the face of a charging lion. It's a tall order to place with Fate but sometimes the fantasy does come true, at least for a few, at least in some way, at least for a while.

Fresh-faced and dressed for the bush in socks, boots, and designer khaki, groups of much younger women and men from overseas, most barely out of their teens, sit around cafe tables talking and joking in a multitude of tongues.

"Mertil Strap? Wer is das? Sie ist Schauspielerin, nicht wahr?"

They're mainly from the USA, Germany, the UK, Holland, or Scandinavia, here to attend weeks- or months-long courses to qualify as game guides. They, more likely their parents, pay handsomely for practical tuition and they're happy with basic accommodation, the kind they'd likely moan like drains about it if it wasn't part of the adventure. Even if they complete the field work and pass the tests, virtually none will go on to work as game guides. There aren't the openings and that was never their intention anyway. They come for an immersive experience, a love of wildlife, a different way of life, to learn skills that will be redundant when they go home to the urban jungle and begin their true careers.

Some Hoedspruit folks are as deeply rooted in the soil as the local leadwood trees. They were born here, they've been here their whole lives, they know where the bones are buried, and the oldest among them like you to know that they know.

They talk of the past with a hint of sadness, deprecation, or with a proud proprietorial air, sometimes all three, mixed emotions, woman or man. You protect what you love.

By and large, they're the grandchildren or great grandchildren of pioneer farmers, because this was farming country and some of it still is closer to the mountains and the water sources: oranges, mangoes, market gardens, even some immunized cattle, safe now that the tsetse flies have gone, and the lions are fenced in. In the past, many of the huge ill-defined farms were used for hunting wild game and to graze cattle but not year-round. Herds would be driven down the mountains from the plateau in autumn and driven back up in spring before the tsetse flies woke up and got into gear again. It was a hard, hot life for men and uncomplaining beasts.

In a wound-down sense this was and still is a military town, home to three squadrons of the South African Air Force, none of which currently have any airworthy aircraft.

It's a long story, involving expensive spares, a distinct lack of imminent invasions, and shrinking budgets. In the 1980s, the airbase east of the town had the notable distinction of being a designated emergency landing site for NASA's Space Shuttles but those heady days are gone. The base now allows its runways to be used by commercial airlines that daily ferry in platoons of foreign tourists transiting Johannesburg, Cape Town, and other parts of South Africa. The airlines have their own busy little terminal at the south end of the runway, a stark contrast to the thumb twiddling presumably going on at the north end where Mirage fighters once tested their engines. But it's a welcome invasion, unlike the one the base was originally built to defend against.

The military share other aging infrastructure and facilities with the Hoedies, including an Olympic-sized swimming pool, tennis courts, and a golf course. Near the top of Mariepskop, the tallest mountain in the nearby Klein Drakensberg, they also left behind what is now a ghost village, spooky as all such places are. Once home to about four hundred military personnel and their families, it's been deserted for over thirty years. The natural vegetation is gradually reclaiming the site, breaking down doors and windows, collapsing roofs, smothering a children's playground, and piling up dead leaves in the corners of empty, roofless bedrooms. War or peace, it's best to play the game, to stay fit, to stop glum thoughts from swirling round and around in the eddies of your mind.

the ugly bug ball

There aren't many songs about bugs—why would there be—but the best of a limited bunch is "The Ugly Bug Ball," first sung by Burl Ives in *Summer Magic*, a Disney film. The lyrics of the song paint a happy picture of bug life, but if you want a good night's sleep, it's probably best not to dwell on what they really get up to.

There were very few bugs about when we moved into the cottage. It was July, mid-winter, and they were either dead, buried, pupating, hibernating or otherwise indisposed. We weren't complaining.

They start to reappear en masse and in endless varieties in October after the first summer rains when the grasses, bushes, and trees energetically burst into life again. That's not a coincidence, of course, because plants and insects have been hanging out with one another for 450 million years, evolving side by side ever since their prototypes first started populating the land. They've had a long time to perfect and synchronize their routines.

The first signal that a protracted ugly bug ball was about to begin in and around the cottage was a spectacular and silent explosion, a translucent eruption rising from the top of a large mound in the moonlight. It looked wonderful, beautiful, and surreal, a psychedelic mushroom cloud silently boiling and evolving until, that is, the blast had time to cover the intervening distance and spoil the effect. The blast came in the form of thousands of flying termites hitting the windows.

They were obviously heading for the light in the lounge so we turned it off, then the TV before they could home in on that and upset the CNN presenters. What is it about bugs and lights in the dark? There are many theories, but nobody seems to have really solved the riddle. When I'm standing in pitch blackness listening to the buzz and waiting for my eyes to adjust to the moonlight, I tend to think about such things. But not for long.

"Did you shut the kitchen window?!" asks a doom-laden voice in the gloom.

"No, I thought you had!"

We turned the light on again and immediately saw that all was not quiet on the Western Front. Marie had forgotten to close the window. I mean one of us had forgotten to close the window. No time to argue about that, there were thousands of termites all over the place, fluttering about or already wingless, carpeting the kitchen, massing on the walls, and advancing on all fronts. Undeterred by this intimidating display of numerical superiority, we waded in with dustpan and brush, plugging breaches left and right, trying to hold the line. Discarded termite wings are lighter than a feather, lighter than a soft sigh, they don't weigh anything. When you try to sweep them up, they assume a life of their own and capriciously take to the air, mocking you with an agility born of nothingness.

Several large termite mounds exploded that evening, so it took a couple of hours for the onslaught to end. By the time we flopped into bed we'd chucked bucket loads of the party goers and their detached appendages out of the window, hoping a couple of passing aardvarks would eat them. Something did because there was no sign of any outside in the morning, just a rippling gossamer carpet of idly drifting wings.

Termites own most of Africa south of the Sahara. They own most of the world. In 2018, the Brazilians discovered an area they apparently hadn't noticed before, as big as the UK, which has 20 million termite mounds. If laid end to end, the tunnels of the world's termites, below and above ground, would probably reach Pluto. Not that any of them would want to go there given the distinct lack of untreated timber.

I need to digress for a moment and talk about poo, it won't take long.

The entire landscape here is a toilet as far as wild animals are concerned, but they do have favorite spots, our driveway being one of them. I see leopard scat, giraffe droppings, which look like unappealing bunches of black grapes, and the scattered squishy marble-sized poos of impalas, the most prolific poopers. The impalas have a territorial marker thing going on halfway down the driveway and it's frequently refreshed, so to speak. But the biggest contributors by sheer volume are elephants. When they're walking up or down the driveway, they seem to have only one thing on their mind.

My point is that this bounteous supply of poo attracts

lots of dung beetles, not to mention battalions of other bugs with varying agendas. The dung beetles fly in from all around but seem to especially favor an eastern approach: up the driveway with the morning sun at their back. They fly in at a height of 1.81 meters which is exactly where the middle of my face is when I go for my morning walk. My Uncle Toby flew a bomber in WWII, dodging anti-aircraft flak until he could dodge no more, and I remember him as I weave to and fro, shrugging off the occasional hit on my forehead or my chin in the interests of winning the war against sloth.

Dung beetles do provide an essential service, tidying up the dung into balls so they can roll it away and bury it. They must downsize the big lumps of elephant poo and upscale the impalas' offerings to assemble a ball that's just right for their purposes. There are not many contractors you could persuade to do that.

I suppose spiders also poo but it's not something you especially notice. There are about 50,000 species of spiders in the world. Not all of them live in or around our cottage, but they're reasonably well represented. I don't have a problem with spiders provided they're not abseiling down from the rafters onto my sandwich or the back of my neck. We have a tried and tested method of dealing with them, which doesn't involve stomping, chemical warfare or rolled up newspapers. We use a net on the end of a thin bamboo pole, the same type of kit children use to forage about in tidal pools for minnows, hermit crabs, and other small crustaceans.

We perfected our technique with rain spiders at Hoog in die Takke on the coast years ago, and we've never lived anywhere since without the net. Rain spiders, so called because they tend to come indoors when the clouds are threatening rain (don't we all), can get intimidatingly large, the biggest the size of saucers. They don't spin webs, they're nocturnal hunters, and they rarely bite people. If they do, it's not a medical emergency, but you don't want them exploring your anatomy during the night. My daughter woke up one morning to find herself eyeball to multiple eyeballs with a gigantic specimen sharing her pillow. Young girls don't like it when that happens.

Given a little nudge, spiders big and small aren't averse to climbing into the net. The lattice possibly seems vaguely familiar to them, and once on board they seem to feel safe. I also feel safe because I'm at the other end of a long bamboo pole. They sometimes get so preoccupied with exploring the net and admiring the craftsmanship that went into weaving it that they're hard to shake off outside.

The net also works with scorpions, though not as well. We very rarely find scorpions in the cottage, but one night, two enormous jet-black specimens mysteriously and simultaneously teleported in. They had large pincers and thin tails, not the type to put you in hospital, but enough to create pain and give you the creeps.

I spotted the first one on the floor, apparently waiting for someone to open the front door. I duly obliged and it scuttled out into the night with only a little nudge from a broom. Seconds later Marie shouted that its party date was inspecting her slippers in the bedroom. Getting it into the net was tricky, not helped by Marie issuing instructions from her vantage point on top of a chair. Eventually it retreated into one of the slippers, so I scooped that up with the net and dropped it out of the window with its passenger.

"What? I'll fetch it later."

The ugly bug ball rages on through the summer months but eventually starts to peter out as the sun weakens, the days shorten, and the temperature drops.The number of bugs circling the light on the porch lessens night by night like a disco gradually forsaken by its patrons. After the first prolonged nighttime chill, almost none remain.

rules of the game

"It's not tame, it's a wild animal, follow the rules," the ranger said, fixing a stern eye on my hot pants' older sister for some reason. He'd obviously marked me as a wimpy kid but had doubts about her. Insulting.

That was in the early 1960s. A large bull elephant with impressive tusks habitually visited an unfenced safari lodge in northern Uganda we sometimes stayed at. He didn't come every day, but most days. He stood on the lawn in the shade of a big baobab tree for hours on end, always alone and always seemingly lost in his own elephantine thoughts.

We were told the elephant had followed the same routine for several months, threatening no one, doing nothing, scarcely moving for hours on end. He'd even made it onto the front page of the lodge's latest brochure. Nothing advertises a wild stay better than a gigantic bull elephant under a baobab with a handsome couple sipping cocktails in the foreground.

What probably had to happen did happen. A new guest arrived, know-it-all, large and loud. He ignored the warnings and walked right up to the elephant, stopped within touching distance, and turned to grin at his wife so she could take a happy snap with her Kodak Box Brownie camera. Without fuss or warning, the elephant picked her husband up with its trunk, shook him like a rattle, and then threw him at the baobab. It then ambled away as though nothing had happened.

There was a lot of commotion, weeping, and wailing after that. I'm not sure whether rangers went after the elephant. They may have gone through the motions but the visitor had brought it on himself so there was no sensible reason for the elephant to die too.

We are often asked about lethal animal encounters in and around Hoedspruit. Some people expect we'll respond with a long list of gory stories, like the one above. I suppose that's fair enough, with so many human beings living in unfenced spaces cheek-by-jowl with wild animals, the body count ought to be spectacular.

But it isn't. There are incidents of course. Last year two Air Force personnel were briefly attacked by a leopard when they were walking between houses in the staff village. Both were badly lacerated but survived. The year before that, a mother pushing her son in a pram in the Blyde Valley Estate was attacked by a giraffe and both were seriously injured. The leopard turned out to be old and injured, while the giraffe had just given birth. Extenuating circumstances, in a way...

That's about it, although not every incident makes the papers and wild animals are, of course, unpredictable. Not only wild animals, any animal, any bird. My mother had a pet parrot, an African Grey who hailed from the Ssese Islands in Lake Victoria, and that was his name—Ssese, not Victoria, though in hindsight it should have been the latter. I still have a scar on my finger to prove just how unpredictable Ssese was, the belligerent little blasphemer. But he loved my mother. She could hold him upside down, cradle him like a baby, tickle him on the tummy and still he kept his beak in check. In fact, he was gentle and friendly with all women, stricter with young girls, and disliked men, boys, and dogs. When he was about twenty years old, he laid an egg, which somehow explained everything and yet nothing. "Disgraceful," Ssese would screech, and in a way I can't possibly explain, she was right.

Law firms trolling for someone to sue in the USA report that about 4.5 million people are attacked by domestic dogs each year, and on average 98 of them die, directly or due to complications. It's a similar proportional picture in the UK. Of course, people aren't expecting to be attacked by their own dog, or even one that's loose on the street, so they're not generally alert to the possibility. There's no reason they should be because most dogs don't bite unless deliberately provoked. What constitutes provocation is decided by the dog. But they're all protective of their owners, and delivering buff envelopes with outrageous bills inside sometimes qualifies as provocation, as mailmen know.

African wild or painted dogs rarely, if ever, attack humans. A photo did the rounds featuring a tourist, whose car had broken down in Kruger Park, standing on a roadside directional pedestal surrounded by a pack of wild dogs. He'd been silly enough to try and walk to find help rather than staying with his vehicle and waiting for somebody to come along. The pedestal was a derisory three feet high, hardly a haven, and the dogs could easily have knocked him off and torn him to bits. Instead, they seemed to find his antics highly amusing.

In all the time we've been living in the cottage, the only animal obviously intent on ridding the world of me was a white rhino. I'd driven to the gate and picked up Marcus, a general fixer who helps us sometimes, and we were nearly home. We saw three rhinos in a curving stretch of the road, but I paid them no mind until Marcus banged on the dashboard and yelled at me to "Go! Go! Go!" A glance through the passenger window showed why. One of the rhinos was heading our way, not just warning us off, but head down, horn to the fore and coming at full speed, which can be 50 kph (31 mph) on a good day. He seemed to have worked out where we'd be in the time it would take him to get to the dirt road and only missed the back of the car by inches. Good at trigonometry obviously. I swerved into our driveway moments later, only to be halted by three giraffes blocking the way. I half expected the rhino to recalibrate and ram us in the rear, but he'd disappeared into the bush like an out-of-control steamroller.

I've often wondered why that rhino, one of three, decided we needed to be obliterated. White rhinos are normally placid and ignore vehicles. But we'd passed three lionesses a few hundred meters before and perhaps their proximity had unsettled him. Or maybe it was just one of those dice-rolling days.

If your number's up, a domestic cow can kill you. It's unromantic to go out like that, but it happens, and when it does, everyone struggles to keeps a straight face at the inquest.

Each year a handful of people in the UK get killed by cows. In the USA, its four or five handfuls. The statistics are vague, but they do meander into a meadow of double figures. Interestingly, cows, not bulls, invariably commit the deadly deed.

Having a dog with you when you're walking across a field ups your chances of a cow attack by about fifty to sixty percent, maybe more. Sorry, the statisticians who normally handle this stuff are all out to lunch. Cows, especially cows with calves, see a dog as a predator so they go on the offensive. If you're ambling through the meadow by yourself, they'll assume you're the village idiot and leave you alone, but dog walkers try and protect their pets, forgetting that their four-legged friend can run much faster than they can. That's a potentially injurious or fatal mistake. The best advice is to drop the lead and let Fido leg it while you attend to your own survival.

There are no loose dogs wandering the streets of Hoedspruit, instead there are warthogs. Not many on any given day, but the occasional loner, more usually a family—mom, dad, and a couple of kids. They trot through the streets like shoppers on a mission, dodging other pedestrians and road traffic, retreating to the bush when they tire of the hustle and bustle. People leave them alone and they don't really bother anyone. They sneak under a fence somewhere to get to town and when they've seen enough, they know their way home.

But it's a bad idea to assume a warthog is benign, and you don't have to come to Africa to find that out.

An article in *Texas Monthly* tells a gory story about a young man and his pet warthog. He looked after the warthog from its infancy, and they got along well, spending long lazy hours together in the hog's spacious enclosure, the young man often reading and the warthog cuddled up and snoozing with its massive head resting on his thigh. (You probably had to be there to appreciate the coziness of that). Six years went by, the warthog grew a fine set of tusks and put on weight until he eventually tipped the scales at 250 pounds, heavier than Dwayne "The Rock" Johnson.

One day, for no reason anyone was able to discern at the time or has done since, the warthog charged the young man, knocked him down, and did its best to kill him. When it thought it had, it wandered away and, despite being badly mangled and punctured by the warthog's teeth and tusks, the young man took the opportunity to crawl out of the enclosure and call for help. Nineteen operations later he was again able to walk.

Stories like that are legion, with the warthog easily replaced in the narrative by a lion, a tiger, a leopard, a hippo or any other wild animal that grows up in captivity and suddenly has an epiphany: I'm not human, I'm not a pet, and if this biped reads one more chapter of that drivel out loud, there are going to be hospital bills to pay.

friends and distant neighbors

If you're stranded alone on a desert island, it's easy to make imaginary friends. In *Cast Away*, Tom Hanks gets to know a volleyball called Wilson. Even though Wilson is a piece of sports equipment, the two become inseparable friends. Wilson puts on such a convincing performance that cinema audiences shed tears when he's swept away in a storm, leaving behind the distraught buddy who had kept him inflated with idle chatter.

Living in a wildlife estate, especially a big one with lions and elephants, isn't the same as being on a desert island, but if you push the metaphor to its creaking outer limits, there are similarities. There's a fence around the boundaries of the estate, not the same as a beach, but it does stop most animals escaping and waves of poachers from flooding in. Within this wild paradise, people build houses that blend in and are well hidden from their neighbors. When complete, it should be possible to stroll out onto the wooden deck like Robinson Crusoe, gaze over the bushes and trees at the far horizon, see no human structure, and imagine you're the sole survivor. Then, like a puff of smoke appearing where it shouldn't, the cell phone beeps, and you know you're not; you're sharing the place with a tribe of crazy people.

"The Birds are back in their nest!" the WhatsApp message bellows.

A couple of minutes silence and the phone beeps

again.

"You mean the vultures," reads the next message.

A catastrophic social gaff. The message is from someone new to the estate unfamiliar with Mr. and Mrs. Bird. The Birds are good people, not known for picking at carcasses. They've had extensive renovations going on at their house and kept group members up to date with every twist and turn, every wrong-sized screw, every blunder in the building process. The job is now done, the subject picked clean, the contractor's bones are bleaching in the sun.

Living in the bush, far from noise and neighbors and the hustle and bustle of city life, the trivial can take on Wilsonian importance. Throw social media into the mix and every minor domestic event, every hiccup in routine, every irritant becomes a news event worthy of broadcasting to the world, or at least the shrunken version of the world the broadcaster is living in.

To be fair, that's not just a feature of bush living, it's the same in all gated communities, especially those where the average age is the arthritic side of fifty. Before the advent of cell phones and social media, and gated communities for that matter, people only had two direct neighbors, one on each side. If it turned out the one in the middle was a looney, the other two could immediately make a dash for the door when the crazy old grouch came shambling out to hang up washing or mow the lawn. Now there's no escape. Cell phones and social media have plugged the irascible, the gloomy, and the just plain mad into a much wider audience.

Our estate's WhatsApp social group is generally a happy place, jumping from topic to topic, friendly banter back and forth, bragging answered with begrudging praise, but every now and again somebody takes offense at a joke, a meme, or a chance remark. It doesn't happen often but when it does, the mood darkens and the exchanges rapidly escalate to the edge of apoplexy. In the climactic moments before a moderator starts frantically jabbing the delete button, it's easy to visualize bared teeth, faces contorted with rage, and realize that our species hasn't moved as far from its primate roots as we like to fondly imagine.

Which brings us of course to baboons. The Baboon Group is always active during the day, as are the baboons. This is a real-time WhatsApp virtual war room, humans versus their cunning distant cousins. Baboon movements are plotted by direct observation and cameras mounted on the walls of houses. Instead of flashy monikers like "Eagle Eye" and "Nemesis," group members use their property number to convey their observation point and report enemy musters and movements. The flashy monikers were tried of course but they met with so much derision that they were quickly abandoned.

"M15: chased off a large troop, they're heading north."

"M16: Not again. Any chance you can chase them south for a change?"

Probably not. The baboons go where the fancy takes them. They can go deeper into the bush, away from houses, or hop over the fence into a neighboring reserve and raise human hackles there. But why should they bother when M12, known to baboon spies to be a heavy shopper, hasn't been home for a couple of days and has flimsy latches on his windows and doors, no cameras on the walls, and a full fridge.

Baboons have their own surveillance systems, they never miss a trick, and a full-scale baboon home invasion can be a disaster. They don't just raid the fridge, they sometimes tip it over, rip the TV off the wall, break furniture, shred fabrics and, as a final gesture of utter contempt, leave strategically placed poo landmines for the returning homeowner. It's a war that will never end, vicious at times, declared when the primate tree was still a sapling.

The cameras on the walls don't just pick up baboons of course. Sometimes the alarm goes out that a human being is in a place he shouldn't be. The first photo posted is indistinct, bad lighting, the camera's view obscured by bushes. It could be a poacher, maybe Big Foot. The next is a video, crystal clear, he's out in the open. It's a muscular young man in a cap wearing impossibly tight shorty shorts walking mysteriously through the shadowy bush, stopping now and again to search for something in a patch of undergrowth.

"M15: Does anybody know who this is?"

"M20: Those shorts are outrageous, how was that allowed on the estate."

"M18: It's 38 degrees (100 F). Is there a dress code?"

Messages go back and forth, and it's eventually revealed that there's a water leak. The strange young man is a plumber and he's searching the undergrowth for pipes and taps.

The woman at M18 immediately posts that she has a plumbing problem and would appreciate his cell phone number. The next two posts are quickly deleted.

Idling minds in idle time, triggered into action by a virtual world invented for fun and games, and sometimes rows beyond midnight. We can shut ourselves off at the press of a button but it's best to stay connected. WhatsApp is also used by reserve management for important stuff, including updates on roadworks in the reserve and news about bush fires near and far. Wildfires are the dread of people living in thatched houses, and even more terrifying for their parsimonious insurers.

Some fires are set for a purpose, to clear bush and maintain fire breaks, but it's good to know the smoke you see is controlled not wild. We keep a briefcase for the real thing filled with personal treasures, permissions to live and travel, proof of who we are and have always been, compliance certificates issued and reissued year on year for a fee by the faceless and unaccountable. At home the briefcase is locked away, but I cling to it when we travel. Michael calls the briefcase the nuclear codes.

We like to pretend we're ready for Armageddon.

Hoedspruit has a fire brigade, but the different reserves and wildlife estates also quickly come together whenever a bush fire breaks out, bringing their manpower and resources, pumps, and water tankers, unbegrudging help in the heat and acrid smoke. Good neighbors. Everyone remembers the one that got away.

posting hippos

Known only to a select few, the Postal Hippo Club had its headquarters in the bar of a small, ramshackle hotel in northern Uganda, not far from the banks of the White Nile near Murchison Falls. During its brief existence in the late 1950s, the club never had more than seven or eight members. My dad was one of them.

To qualify as a member, an initiate had to stick a postage stamp on the backside of a hippopotamus by the light of the moon. It didn't have to be a full moon, they weren't that mad, just enough moon. Hippos come out of the water to graze at night, so that was the only time they could be stamped.

The method was simple. Members consumed many beers and then climbed aboard a decrepit old Willys Jeep, stripped of its doors and windows, and sallied forth into the night looking for grazing hippos. The objective was for the Jeep to come up alongside an unsuspecting hippo so that the initiate could lean out and stick on a stamp. Not any part of the hippo's anatomy would do, it had to be the bum or as near as dammit. Club members obviously assumed postal authorities would reject improperly stamped hippos.

Hippos don't take kindly to having a postage stamp slapped on their backside and it was only the skill, or more probably the luck of the driver, that saved the Jeep from becoming scrap, and me from becoming an orphan.

My dad never explained why the Club was disbanded. All he would say was that they ran out of stamps, but I suspect the local askaris (African policemen) had something to do with it.

I immediately thought about that Jeep when Michael bought an old game viewer. In its prime it had been a V6 4x4 Mitsubishi Pajero. Now in its dotage, it had undergone a conversion. The roof was missing, cut off at the door sills, and so were the windows. Three rows of bench seats were installed behind the driver and front passenger seats, each a little higher than the one in front. The third and highest row, with the best view, stuck out at the back in midair. The Postal Hippo Club would have been mighty proud of it, as was my father's grandson.

In and around Hoedspruit, game viewers like this dominate the automotive landscape. They're popular because they deliver exactly what their name implies: unimpeded views of animals, birds, and everything else. They can usually carry ten passengers and most of them belong to game lodges or entrepreneurial game guides who specialize in taking tourists into Kruger. Although all are hybrids of various makes of 4x4s, commercial versions are adapted at birth to be what they're intended to be. Some are luxurious, replete with leather seats, high roofs and canvas drops for rare days of wind and rain. Pull-out bars with fridges are fitted into the rear where the trunk would normally be.

Despite my gloomy expectations, the first few

excursions in Michael's green monster went well. It growled like it meant business, managed the mud and rough roads with ease, didn't belch smoke or make alarming metallic noises. It didn't refuse to start on command, that was important. Even the lights worked. Increasingly confident, Michael loaded up the family and a couple of Jemima's young friends and took us all for an evening drive on a seldom used track to the shores of a small lake. There we would watch the sunset, sip drinks, eat snacks, and hopefully see the resident hippos coming out of the water to feed. Finding a good spot facing a setting sun that was already nine-tenths over the horizon, he turned off the engine. The silence was instantly filled with an ominous hiss and steam billowed out from under the hood, a Laurel and Hardy moment.

It was rapidly getting dark, it does that here when the sun goes down, and there was zero chance another vehicle would happen by. The nearest house was probably a couple of miles away in heaven-knows-which direction through thick bush. In that bush, I could picture leopards and lions stretching their muscles and testing their retractable claws as a prelude to a night's slaughter. Cell phone reception was non-existent, screaming wouldn't help, nor would waiting for the radiator to cool off. By then it would be dark and not a good idea to be fiddling under the bonnet with your back to the ink-black bush.

After a brief debate, we decided to make a dash for home before we literally ran out of steam. At least we would hopefully make it to one of the main dirt roads and potential rescue. The first relief was that the motor started and, after that, during the next chunk of eternity and helter-skelter driving, I sent a steady stream of prayers skyward, luckily unimpeded by a roof. I also kept my fingers crossed that the track wouldn't be blocked by elephants or giraffes. Giraffes have a bolshy habit of standing in the road like very tall traffic cops, commanding you stop so they can inspect you and your vehicle in a leisurely and uniquely aloof and arrogant manner. Maybe not that unique, if I pause to think about it.

We made it home and it turned out no damage was done to the motor. The green monster had saved our bacon, so it wasn't called that anymore (it never had been by Michael.) It had earned its place as part of the family. The problem turned out to be a worn seal on the radiator cap and all the steam and hissing had never been as calamitous as it seemed. Nothing does when you're back behind solid walls in bright electric light.

Tourists who arrive by air are usually met at Hoedspruit's little airport by a game viewer, dispatched by the lodge they're booked to stay at. The safari begins right there, at the luggage carousel. The airport terminal itself is in a game reserve that surrounds the military airbase. I assume the runways are fenced off because there are rhinos, giraffes, and many other large and mobile perils to aviation in that reserve.

Not everyone gets picked up at the airport by lodges

with posh names emblazoned in gold letters on the doors of their gleaming game viewers. Some get picked up by long-haired, pot smoking, beer swigging Brian in a game viewer towing a battered trailer full of camping gear.

Depending on the thickness of their wallet, tourists can choose to safari in an ethereal bubble of outrageous luxury, sipping cocktails by a waterhole where even the mosquitos are issued tiny napkins, or they throw caution to the wind and go with Brian and others of his ilk. There is middle ground of course, but people who want to bury themselves in the African bush and learn the intimate details of its unrespectable inhabitants look for someone adept in the mysteries, sunbaked and well-seasoned.

Brian knows the animals, their day and night routines and sometimes dangerous moods. He knows the trees, not just their names but the story of their long lives, their ponderous ultra slow-motion struggles for survival and procreation in drought and rain. People who want to identify the trees on their properties call on him and, if they happen to have a poisonous snake curled up behind a toilet bowl, he'll relocate that too. He cultivates succulents as a sideline, and they prosper under his care.

Anyone can get to know a subject and get to know it well, but a rare few are somehow able to go beyond the facts and figures, to go much, much further than that, to part the veil and reach the inner sanctum where deep mysteries are revealed. I suppose that's what a guru is, a kind of genius, effortlessly dedicated to their field.

One mystery that I've always wanted to have fully revealed is why people driving very slowly or stopped in game reserves in an open game viewer aren't occasionally pounced on by lions and leopards, plucked out of their seats by angry elephants, or strangled with their binocular straps by aggressive baboons. Most game viewers even have a seat on top of the front left wheel arch where a guide precariously sits, checking the passing dirt for tracks when he's not scanning the landscape. Who would want to be that guy? He's teed up like a golf ball waiting to be whacked.

Brian would know the answer and I asked him. He opened his mouth but was pre-empted by Dipak, a fellow guest, a rich young marketing man on holiday from London who knew a lot about everything, especially Ferraris. He loudly explained that animals see the vehicle and the people in it as one unit, too big to be trifled with.

"And," he quickly added, as Brian began to open his mouth again, "all they can smell is diesel fumes."

Our weary leader shrugged and walked away to check the steaks on the fire.

Elephants and rhinos do sometimes put a dent in a game viewer, if a driver doesn't read the signs and reacts too slowly, but such incidents are very rare. Nobody knows what wild animals think when they encounter a multi-headed metal monster, but they're used to game viewers in game reserves and usually don't take much notice, even when one stops beside them. Experience has taught them that vehicles are pretty much stuck to the road and aren't a threat. But they see the people sitting there, they're not stupid. They react instantly if anyone stands up or waves their arms and immediately run away or get aggressive. If Dipak were to somehow lose his balance and fall out, lions, leopards, and anything else nearby would immediately pick up a whiff of his spectacular deodorant and run for their lives.

the park next door

Any sensible, well-balanced, and relatively law-abiding individual should take about thirty minutes to drive from our cottage to Orpen, the nearest gate into the Kruger National Park. It takes us about fifteen minutes longer than that because we always U-turn after a few hundred yards to pick up Marie's handbag/ sunglasses/ water bottle/ cell phone/ purse/ binoculars/ hat/ not that hat/ the blue hat. To be fair, it's my job to go through the checklist, don't ask me why, and I always fail miserably in that one simple task.

For much of the way, the road to the Orpen gate runs along the southern boundary of Timbavati, made famous in the 1960s by the startling appearance of white lions. They're not albinos; their whiteness is due to a rare gene carried in just the right proportion by both their normal parents, so they come and go over time like the ghosts they resemble.

There's a fair chance we'll see wild animals close to the fence, ten million to one it will be a white lion, but maybe a giraffe, an elephant, a buffalo, or something else. Failing that, we can count on stray cows wandering onto the road. The wide verges seem to be good cattle country. The cowherd is either sitting in the shade of a knob thorn tree or chatting to his girlfriend on the phone, probably both.

Kruger National Park turns one hundred years old in

2026, not as old as Yellowstone but old nonetheless, and one of the biggest parks in Africa. It's about the size of Israel, a little smaller than New Jersey. Over a period of thirty years, starting in the late 1890s, in stops and starts, the park gradually came together, championed by determined and colorful characters. I'll tell you the story.

We may as well start in a room full of severed heads. The room is in the Great North Museum in Newcastle-upon-Tyne in England which houses many other more conventional historical artifacts, treasures, oddities, and curiosities. Most of the heads, all well over a hundred years old but still in pristine condition, originally belonged to Abel Chapman, successful businessman, trophy hunter, writer, and keen naturalist. He was a school and lifelong friend of Frederick Selous, after whom the Selous Game Reserve in Tanzania, the largest in Africa, was named.

It's easy to sneer at historical characters like Abel Chapman, a great white hunter of yore and a bosom buddy of red-faced, mustachioed British colonialists, but lampooning the long dead can be unfair. Abel wasn't just a head collector; he was a conservationist of note.

On a trophy hunt in the Lowveld in 1900, Chapman was shocked by the decimation of wildlife in the area. Unembarrassed by his own small and selective contribution to the slaughter, he submitted a report to the International Convention for the Preservation of Wild Animals which promptly adopted it and later shared it with the British colonial administration in the Transvaal.

The detailed report proposed that a game reserve be established, extending from the Limpopo River in the north to the Crocodile River in the south, bounded by the Lebombo Mountains in the east and the Klein Drakensberg Mountains in the west. Those are close to the boundaries of today's Kruger National Park.

About two years before Chapman sent in his ambitious proposal, Paul Kruger, President of the Transvaal Republic, had proclaimed the Gouvernements Wildtuin. This "wild garden" comprised 4,662 square kilometers of virgin bush between the Crocodile and Sabie rivers, what is now the southern quarter of the park. Izak Holtzhausen, a police sergeant stationed at Crocodile Bridge, was told to keep an eye on it. He probably wasn't over the moon about that, and even less so when the Eastern Transvaal promptly became a war zone.

The Anglo-Boer War started in 1898, and it was soon obvious that the new reserve couldn't become a practical reality amid such mayhem. From October 1899 to May 1902, Boer and British troops contesting the area took time off from shooting at each other to shoot countless animals for the pot. It's worth noting that the local lions hit back as best they could, notching up a modest tally of inattentive combatants and poachers. Sergeant Holtzhausen couldn't do anything about any of it and had probably resigned and joined a Boer commando when the fighting started.

One man who could do something, and did, was

Major Greenhill-Gardyne of the Gordon Highlanders, second-in-command of an unconventional, if not downright bizarre, British-aligned small military force called Steinaecker's Horse, which operated erratically in the Lowveld and along the Moçambique border.

Greenhill-Gardyne (get used to the hyphens, there are more to come) had developed a keen interest in nature and wildlife conservation when he was stationed in India. Like Abel Chapman, who he may have known, he was also alarmed by the rate at which wildlife in the Lowveld was being killed, not only by soldiers, his own and others, but also by poachers, many of whom operated from over the border in Moçambique, exploiting the chaos to set snares on an industrial scale. He did much to reduce the slaughter, earning himself the nominal award of "least liked man in the Lowveld."

When the war ended in 1902, he submitted his own report on the urgent need for proper conservation measures in the Lowveld to the new British administration in the Transvaal, headed by Lord Alfred Milner, himself a keen naturalist.

The upshot of these reports, and many entreaties from other passionate voices, was the proclamation of the Sabie Game Reserve. It followed Paul Kruger's earlier proclamation of the Wildtuin four years previously, matching it virtually word for word, rock for rock, and tree for tree.

You've probably noticed that many of the people

intent on securing a safe space for wildlife in the Lowveld were military men and they had one other thing in common: they were all keen hunters, including Kruger himself. It was that hobby which connected them to the bush, engendered their profound love for it, and their admiration of the animals that lived there.

The man chosen to take charge of the Sabie Game Reserve and told to "Go down there and make yourself disagreeable to everyone" (apparently the main qualification for the job) was also a hunter and a military man, Major James Stevenson-Hamilton, who was appointed first Warden in 1902 and remained so until his retirement in 1946 at the age of 75.

Stevenson-Hamilton seems to have had a blueprint in his head from his first day on the job. Perhaps he'd also read Abel Chapman's detailed report and that inspired his determination to "go big or go bust." He knew that wild animals need their own space and plenty of it to live their lives as nature intended. They couldn't compete for resources with people or their livestock.

One of his first acts was to kick everyone out of the Sabie reserve, including Tsonga herders and hunters, who promptly nicknamed him "Skukuza," meaning "he who sweeps clean" in their language. It wasn't meant as a compliment, but over the ensuing years, he formed close friendships among the Tsonga and earned their respect. Many were employed in the reserve as rangers and game guards as they were experts in bushcraft and taught Stevenson-Hamilton much of what he knew. He grew old as they grew old, and in the end, when he died at the ripe old age of ninety, the tribal elders honored him as a great man. Stevenson-Hamilton would probably have liked that accolade above all the others he received in his long life.

Skukuza, as we'll call him for the moment in solidarity with the Tsongas and to catch a break from hyphens, was a canny Scotsman and he knew the subtle art of getting something for nothing. But he was also lucky, especially in terms of the people who backed his vision at critical moments in the Park's embryonic years. They notably included Jan Smuts and Piet Grobler, grandnephew of Paul Kruger, who, as Minister of Lands, finally pushed through the National Parks Bill in 1926. There's symmetry in that.

In the long lead up to the proclamation, Skukuza had persuaded many landowners to grant him game management rights over their vast estates north of the Sabie River; in effect that meant lending the land, in the sense of lending a book you know you'll probably never get back again. Most farms and estates were owned by companies, including some with titular mining rights, but the directors saw little prospect of profit to be made from their vast tracts of prickly bush. Individual landowners, including the Orpen family, also donated farms and, bit by bit, Skukuza put together a jigsaw that eventually linked up with the Shingwedzi Game Reserve in the far north (also under his control) to complete the picture of the Kruger National Park you'll see today in maps and brochures.

That jigsaw is in fact still being added to. In comparatively recent years fences have dropped between the huge private reserves near Hoedspruit that share borders with Kruger so that wild animals can now move freely to and fro.

In the early years of the Sabie Game Reserve it didn't occur to Stevenson-Hamilton that it could be opened to visitors. To be fair, he had just finished kicking people out and the notion was ridiculous. He did think that controlled hunting might be allowed at some vague future date when animal numbers had reached sustainable levels, but the notion of hordes of day-trippers and overnighters whooping it up in the bush with campfires and picnic hampers didn't enter his head.

An ice-cold beer on a very hot day changed that. His drinking companion, an innkeeper in the small border village of Komatipoort, asked what the point of the reserve was and—answering his own question—said that it would presumably soon be open for shooting.

"What goal were we striving for?" Stevenson-Hamilton later wrote. "It did seem a waste of time and money, if all the labor and care of the past three years was merely to provide meat and hides for the local public."

The result of this introspection was a determination to strive for more, to get the reserve proclaimed a National Park, belonging to all South Africa's people. Nobody could then abuse it or take it away. As we've seen, it was a goal that took another two decades to achieve. Mindful of the continual rumbling discontent from some politicians and various commercial interests, Stevenson-Hamilton knew that any hope of achieving this meant having the tax-paying public firmly on his side, and the only way to achieve that was to open the gates and let them in.

It began cautiously at first, limited numbers, with overnight visitors finding themselves in tents and then mud huts, the kind of spartan accommodation you'd expect from a military man on a tight budget who lived a simple life himself. But people loved the experience, they loved being immersed in the bush, the thrill of lions roaring in the night, of the unexpected, the wonder of seeing wild animals living their primordial lives and meeting their primordial and invariably bloody ends.

Some loved it so much that they wanted everything to stay the same, to stay "authentic." Each improvement was met with mutters and moans and that has continued to the present day. In 1965, the main roads in the park began to be tarred. In the decades before that, a heated debate raged, pitting dust lovers against free breathers, fathers against sons, husbands against wives, and Stevenson-Hamilton against everyone who supported such a silly and dangerous notion. He argued that tarring the roads would inevitably lead to speeding and the consequence would be animals mown down on a catastrophic scale.

He needn't have worried, not about the modest numbers

of people in the early years, nor the vast majority of the two million people who visit the park today. They keep to the speed limit of 50 kph, usually driving slower than that, stopping and starting in response to sightings of birds and animals. The excitement and anticipation, then as now, is tempered by a sense of reverence. Most folk behave as though they're guests in Eden, talking quietly around their campfires, hushed tones in a cathedral of natural wonder.

We regularly visit Kruger and have done so virtually every year for the past fifty years, Marie and her family a lot longer than that. Transported back to six years old, she remembers a potty under a metal-framed bed with noisy springs, an enamel basin, a jug of water, rippling canvas, and shadows dancing together by candlelight. Lacking a fridge, her mom kept butter fresh by wrapping it in a damp cloth and hanging it outside to catch the passing breeze. More than once hyenas or monkeys helped themselves.

Even though we now live in the bush surrounded by the same trees and the same wild animals, we still feel as though a big weight has been lifted when we drive through the Kruger Park gates. I don't claim to be Atlas, or even a distant relation, but in our day-to-day lives, we all carry part of the weight of the worried world our species has created. In Kruger, we get to put that baggage down for a while, to feel a little lighter, a little more innocent. I like to imagine Mother Nature as a grandma, this is her house, this is where she's always lived.

things fall apart

Not content with being one of the greatest statesmen of the twentieth century, Winston Churchill fancied himself as a bricklayer. With his own hands, he built a short wall at Chartwell, his country house in England, and it's still standing, or it was in the mid-1980s. I can vouch for that because we did the estate tour, by chance following behind a professional bricklayer and his family as it turned out.

"Blimey," the bricklayer said as we all stood and stared blankly at the wall. "Just as well we won the war, he didn't know nuffing about bricklaying."

He went on to explain some of the elementary principles of the builder's trade to his disinterested wife and bemused young son.

"We best get on, or we'll miss the bus," his wife interrupted, looking at her watch.

DIY isn't for everyone which is why we rely on Marcus. Marcus comes in every now and again to keep the sickle bush at bay, climbs ladders, fixes ladders, fixes cracks, fixes them again, replaces decking, plasters and paints, among a myriad other tasks. When you ask Marcus if he can do something, he always says yes, even if it sometimes turns out to be no. He was part of the crew who built the cottage and before that Michael's house, so he does know a thing or two and is often keen to experiment with three and four. We can't do without him, except when he fixes something that didn't need mending.

It took me a long time to wake up to the fact that things fall apart. Taken at face value, physical things, especially houses, seemed everlasting to me as a child. When I was young, even old buildings like castles looked as though they'd been there forever and would just carry on, knights in shining armor swopped for tourists in floral shirts, a stone missing here and there but otherwise intact. People grew old and died but things went on forever. That probably explains why I'm hopeless at maintaining houses, castles, and all sorts of other stuff.

Maybe it's something to do with being born in Africa where the idea of maintaining things used to be a foreign concept, and still is among some people. Living a contented life in much of Sub-Saharan Africa used to be relatively simple: nature provided the essentials, all of them recyclable, and there never used to be an obsession with things. When a wattle-and-daub hut began to disintegrate, the whole village pitched in and a replacement was built. The old hut returned to the earth, recycled by termites, baked by the sun, and eventually pummeled back into the raw red earth by heavy rain.

A modern house costs a fortune to build, and an owner's hope and expectation is that it's value will rise, but only if it is scrupulously maintained. More than that, it must be adapted and altered to keep pace with changing trends. Hoedies are as obsessed as everyone else with keeping up with the Joneses. The original Joneses seem to have been characters in a cartoon strip published in *The New York Globe* in the early part of the last century; cartoon characters or not, the pace they set for social climbers has never slowed.

When our cottage was brand new, I thought we could relax for a good long time without worrying about fixing anything; about four months later, cracks had started to appear, and I struggled to open the front door. It had been stiff from day one but now I had to kick my way out. I asked Marcus whether he could fix it.

"Yes," he said confidently, and immediately began unscrewing the door hinges.

Marcus is in his early twenties, so life hasn't had time to convince him that everything is not always as it seems.

He sanded a lot of wood off the inside edge and eventually, after much puffing and panting, we managed to put the door back again. It was worse than before, so we had a joint head scratching session for a minute or two. I even took my hat off so my brain could cool down and let me focus. Then Marcus started tapping around the wooden door frame and I joined in. One section sounded hollow and sure enough it was. His finger poked through the solid looking wood as though it was frosted icing on a soggy cake.

"Termites," he said confidently.

Termites don't mark their workspace with plastic orange cones and red and white tape. When they're busy eating their way through a door frame, or any other wood, they leave a thin veneer to protect themselves from the light and from being discovered. It's a neat trick that some pie makers have copied to hide the fact that the content of their meat pies is not what the pastry suggests.

It took a professional carpenter, assisted by Marcus, a couple of days to sort out the front door. They replaced the frame with properly treated timber, and for the next few days it swung happily to and fro and then began sticking again. Some doors are a pain in the butt and never learn how to behave.

A week later, I discovered the roof was leaking directly above the couch, a sacred space where I sometimes sit to contemplate the meaning of life but mostly to check what's on TV. I was sitting there contemplating when I felt a plop on my head. That was it, a solitary drip. Surprising too, because it hadn't rained for weeks. I looked up at the thatch, heard a faint rustle, and it dawned on me that a bushbaby had just pissed on my head.

A week previously, a bushbaby had set up home in one of the outdoor gas geysers. Marie began running a bath, the geyser fired up, and the bushbaby shot out of the chimney like a little furry cannon ball. He sat there with an indignant look on his tiny face, waiting for things to cool off. In a matter of minutes, he dived back in again. What an idiot, and a relief that our forebears had the good sense to evolve a bit further than that.

Marcus took the geyser off the wall with the bush nuisance still on board, carried it into the long grass, and left it on the ground so its passenger would get the message and find another home. He retrieved it the following morning and, as expected, the bushbaby had gone, but I was astonished by the shrubbery he had managed to stuff inside to make his cozy nest. If Marie hadn't quickly turned off the hot tap when she spotted him shoot out of the chimney, the whole lot might have ignited and spread fire to the thatch above.

The bushbaby probably headed to our rafters during the night when he realized the geyser had temporarily been turned into a little bungalow in the grass, easily accessible to all kinds of carnivorous creatures. Safely ensconced up there in the thatch, I expect it gave him great satisfaction to score a direct hit on my bald patch. I asked Marcus whether he could fix it and he uncharacteristically shrugged his shoulders; he'd done his part.

I'd read somewhere that Gloucestershire airport in the UK had tried playing loud music to scare birds away from their runway and wondered whether that would work on a bushbaby in the thatch. Trial and error at the airport had shown that Tina Turner songs, particularly, "Simply the Best," blasted out at full volume had the desired effect on birds. They hated it, so I decided to give it a try. Nope, our lodger was obviously a big fan because he's still up there and seems to have invited others to join the rave.

When the first heavy rains came, we discovered we really did have leaks in the roof, three of them to be precise. We named them Niagara, Victoria, and Angel Falls so that we knew which one we were talking about. Their sources all seemed to be at or close to the apex. Two were soon bad enough to fill a couple of buckets each during a heavy thunderstorm. I eventually asked Marcus whether he could climb up and see what he could see. He said yes of course, but it wasn't an easy expedition, given the pitch of the roof. The problem turned out to be gaping cracks and holes in the cement cap that's supposed to seal the thatch along the ridge. Marcus tossed down a sizeable chunk and it exploded on the ground like a grey snowball.

It turned out the thatching contractor who had originally done the work, and with great fanfare given the five-year guarantee, had gone out of business. I didn't need to wonder why.

About a year after we'd moved in, various appliances started exhibiting peculiar signs of distress. The washing machine started dancing and made unusual gurgling noises, the kettle started screaming like a banshee, the shower head began spraying water all over the place, except on me directly underneath, and the water pressure pump started to rattle like bones bouncing on a tin roof. I chalked it up to a poltergeist infestation, and the real problem turned out to be chalk of a sort, enormous deposits of calcium from the borehole water. According to the exorcist working at the hardware store, I was supposed to change the filter and put in weird and expensive transparent balls every few months to sort out the calcium overload. His incredulity left little doubt I was the ineptest specimen of a DIY homeowner he'd ever come across.

"Domkop," I heard him whisper to the girl at the cash register. That's as bad as it sounds, but I've never claimed to be Winston Churchill.

night shift

When you see a sign for a bar called "Sleepers," it's natural to assume that the person who chose that name was inspired by the comatose bodies strewn across the floor, the furniture, and hanging out of windows in the sweet crisp light of morning. It would be that kind of place, the sort you should only visit in the daytime, before the previous night's patrons had sobered up and made bail.

Then again, the name might refer to railway sleepers. That's different, a different kind of place. Bars and restaurants in converted railway stations, especially where the rails outside are still in regular use, have an atmosphere imbued with pathos and romance. Whether you like it or not, someone starts singing "The Way We Were" inside your head as you step over the threshold. Airports used to have a similar leaving-on-a-jet-plane romantic vibe, but that's been blotted out by a seething mass of humanity burdened with too much baggage.

Sleepers is a popular restaurant in Hoedspruit, popular with both locals and tourists. Not just the bar, more so the restaurant, and it's been around a long time. Guests can enjoy breakfast, lunch or a leisurely dinner and it's unlikely they'll find themselves in the middle of a brawl between red-faced men with white knuckles settling old scores.

Substantially unchanged, the building used to be the town's railway station, of course, but no scheduled trains have stopped here to pick up or drop off passengers for decades. The Blue Train is occasionally chartered to bring wealthy tourists from Pretoria to Hoedspruit. They detrain against the background tinkle of empty champagne glasses being returned to a waiter's tray and are promptly ferried to luxurious lodges of their choice.

Goods trains also sometimes stop, but only for operational reasons, not to take on cargo. Wagons are pushed and pulled, clashing against each other like impatient giants in a queue; shouts in the dark, a whistle blows, and the assembled train lurches forward, slowly gathering speed, for the long haul to a distant destination on the coast.

Sleepers and the other restaurants around town mainly cater for the breakfast, lunch, and early supper trade. Dining late into the night is rare because most people go to bed early here and get up early, tourists to be ready for a pre-dawn game drive, staff even earlier to cater for their needs. In the long summer months, workers, walkers, joggers, and even the indolent are up before dawn to take advantage of the cooler air.

The town begins to surrender the streets soon after sunset. Shops and cafes close and the last few minibus taxis depart, taking the stragglers home; the number of pedestrians dwindles until there are none. By ten o'clock, the night shift furtively takes over: a family of porcupines cautiously rattles into earshot, perhaps a genet or a civet cat, even the occasional leopard. A series of security cameras mounted on the walls at the brand-new, yet-to-be-opened private hospital caught a leopard leaping a boundary wall, inspecting doors and windows, assessing an unwelcome addition on the periphery of its hunting grounds. The footage made the local paper.

"Good to see the hospital is offering cat scans," quipped a WhatsApp wit.

Driving home in the night to our cottage is often eventful. We trundle along with dimmed headlights, parking lights if the moon is bright, so as not to dazzle the antelope and small night creatures. Herds of antelope often gather on the road, maybe to enjoy the residual rising heat, perhaps because they feel safer in the open.

Humans aren't built for the dark. We don't see well, no matter the number of carrots our mothers told us to eat. Whatever abruptly appears in the small pool of light ahead of the car—a nightjar, a springhare, or a mouse—catches us by surprise. Our biggest surprise to date has been a couple of elephants copulating in the road. Surprises don't come bigger than that. Lacking a daytime sense of scale and distance, the colossal apparition filled the windscreen to overflowing by the time I registered what I was looking at. The decent thing was to reverse and give them some privacy, but that option was immediately cancelled by other elephants stepping into the road behind us. Maybe they'd assumed we had the best view and were jostling for position. In the interests of common decency, I turned off the lights, a move that was greeted with shuffles and rumbles of disappointment from the voyeurs at the back.

Apart from that-kind-of-thing, as my mother used to refer to procreative matters, the night is a busy place in the bush around us. It's also an invisible place. On moonless nights there is very little sky glow because the nearest big towns are far away, and Hoedspruit itself gets by with only a handful of lamp posts. The land is pitch black and the stars are consequently amazing on cloudless nights. Living here, you soon realize how silent the world is without humanity's forest of lights and incessant noises. But it's never totally quiet. There are rustles, squeaks, and screeches, and every now and again a bloodcurdling grunt, howl, or full-throated roar. Noises in the dark leave a lot to the imagination.

Lions are usually at their most vocal during the night, but they've got class, so they don't overdo it. We hear them roaring at dusk or later in the night when they're co-ordinating their hunt and we're tucked up in bed. They're usually far away but sometimes right outside. When they are right outside, being inside, tucked up in bed clutching a pillow, doesn't make you feel much safer.

The sound has been likened to all sorts of other loud noises, including a rock concert and a jet plane at full throttle, but none of these man-made comparisons do it justice. At close quarters, a lion's roar can reach a decibel level that causes pain, but it's not about the volume, rather the menacing and primal authority it conveys. There are gruesome lessons buried in our species' past, not too deeply, that make us tremble when we hear it.

Lions roar for a variety of reasons—to keep in touch with other members of their pride, to warn off potential rivals, or simply to let every living thing within a five-mile radius know that this is their patch and they won't put up with back chat.

Everything else might be impressed but not spotted hyenas. They regard a lion's roar, if not as a dinner gong, at least as an indication of where dinner might soon be served. Hyenas have their own repertoire of dawn-world noises, ranging from grunts, yelps, whoops, and howls to their infamous cackle. You're most likely to hear that at the feeding frenzy around a kill in the dead of night, a gruesome context that makes their apparent hilarity sound demonic. It's a group thing, triggered by a mixture of excitement and fear, and they don't really find dismembered corpses hysterically funny. At least, I hope not.

Hyenas tend to stay well-hidden during the day so the best chance of seeing one is in the evening or early morning. We often see them around the cottage soon after sunset, usually passing by on their way to somewhere else, or while we're driving home in the dark.

In Kruger Park, as in most other wildlife reserves, visitors aren't allowed to drive around in the dark in their own vehicles. In the early years, it was thought that shining lights at animals was intrusive and would upset the nocturnal natural order. A reasonable assumption, but not one that could stand up to the pressure of human curiosity coupled with the need to generate income for park management and conservation.

Official guided night drives began in the 1970s and within a decade they were firmly on the list of popular add-on activities Kruger offers to visitors at most of their camps. Guests must still be back behind the gates by sunset, but for a fee they can join an official night drive for a different kind of experience, see a different spotlit stage with a new cast of characters.

That's the theory but in my experience animals that stay hidden during the day are even better at staying hidden during the night. It's how they do what they do for a living. As your eyes rotate from side to side and up and down, following the conical white beam of a guide's million candlepower torch, the chances of seeing something are bleak. If you're my age, the chances of ending up with a stiff neck and aching eyeballs are excellent. I have yet to see a pangolin on a night drive, and I've only seen one aardvark; that was twenty years ago, and the driver nearly collided with a tree as he tried to keep the spotlight on the zigzagging little weirdo.

To be fair, an experienced guide wields a spotlight like a surgical instrument, dissecting the dark until he picks up movement, or more usually eyes that reflect the light. It then becomes a tricky balancing act, defusing the beam or aiming the spotlight so that the periphery gives sufficient light to see the animal or bird without dazzling it. Amateurs are not always that thoughtful or careful.

As things stand, official night drives in Kruger invariably end by eight o'clock, as they do in the wildlife reserve we live in, and the dark is then left to the creatures that own it. That, in my unhumble opinion, is as it should be.

shots in the dark

In 1530, during the reign of Henry VIII, English parliamentarians, landed gentry to a man, showed how they felt about poachers by passing The Whipping Act. Whipping posts sprung up in villages and towns all over the country and were frequently used as an example, and a warning. Repeat offenders were hanged, a high price to pay for a rabbit stew.

Given this draconian response, poaching, like smuggling, made its way into modern times still shielded by an aura of romance: Robin Hood and his merry men living off the land and battling the greed and unfair practices of the high and mighty. In recent years, that aura has evaporated like a white mist cloaking a fetid swamp. Poaching in modern Africa is big business, the poachers often better armed and equipped than the gamekeepers. They're not hunting for the pot but to top up the burgeoning bank balances of crime bosses thousands of miles away, mainly in Southeast Asia; they target rhinos and pangolins, and anything else that features in the high-priced pharmacopeia of mad medicine.

Kruger National Park and the game reserves around Hoedspruit are on the front line in this seemingly never-ending battle against poachers. The fight is against thugs and gangsters armed with automatic weapons and high-tech equipment rather than merry men in green tights with bows and arrows. To counter them, conservationists have fielded tough hombres of their own, joined in recent years by equally tough and highly trained dogs.

We see little of this in our cozy cottage in the bush, but on a visit to northern Kruger, we had a rare encounter with two weary men in battle gear with rifles, sitting by a road junction a bit beyond nowhere; they looked more like Navy Seals than traditional game rangers. They told us they'd been on foot patrol for three weeks, covering a vast swathe of the park and this was their pickup point. I asked whether they'd come across any poachers.

One of them nodded and then replied with an ambiguous smile. "No more bullets," he said.

We sometimes see a K-9 anti-poaching unit on patrol in the reserve where we live. There haven't been any poaching incidents in the past few years, and the patrols are the reason for that.

A two-man unit came to our rescue once. An elephant bull had seemed intent on knocking over the platform holding up our array of solar panels. We park our car under that, so the situation had the potential to become a double disaster. He kept testing one of the six thick wooden poles holding up the platform; to this day its slightly banana shaped.

No amount of Marie shouting "voetsek" seemed to deter him. In a panic, I considered chucking salvos of apples and oranges but decided that was a daft idea. I'd quickly run out of ammunition, and he might get the wrong idea, that the bombardment was a reward, and re-double his efforts to crack the pillar once he'd eaten the fruit. Before I could do anything that stupid, the rangers responded. It only took them a couple of minutes, as they'd fortunately been passing nearby. One look at them and their no-nonsense dog and the elephant high-tailed it off into the bush, trumpeting indignantly. I think he'd met them before. They told me an elephant, probably the same one, had wrecked the solar panels at a house a couple of miles away. He'd got it into his head that such things simply didn't belong. Who can say he's wrong.

Visitors to Hoedspruit can witness the impact poaching has on wildlife and be introduced to some of the survivors in one of the nearby animal rehabilitation centers. Some specialize in rescuing and rehabilitating endangered species, such as cheetahs and rhinos. Others, like Moholoholo Wildlife Rehabilitation Centre, take in a wide spectrum of injured wild animals and birds from all over the country. They're not all orphaned or injured in poaching incidents, some have been hit by cars, others have flown into power lines or been struck by the propellor of an eco-dubious giant windmill. Others needed rescuing for a multitude of other reasons, virtually all related to interactions with humans and/or one of their inventions.

Moholoholo is home to Stoffels, a honey badger made famous on TV and YouTube for being a bright spark with an uncanny ability to escape from the enclosures built to keep him out of harm's way. He can't be released into the wild because he was rescued as a young pup forlornly trotting along the gutter of a suburban road in the Cape and is now too imprinted on humans to successfully make his own way in the wide wild world. We took Jemima along to make his acquaintance.

As befits the star of the show, the tour guide left Stoffels until last. I won't give you an exhaustive list of what we saw; it included two white lions and a black leopard that stared at Jemima as though she was the one personally responsible for his incarceration. Maybe she just looked like a potential lunch, but the unblinking stare had enough heat to melt her ice cream.

Next was a capacious aviary housing a variety of raptors and vultures that had run into trouble, usually in the form of poisoned carcasses set by poachers hired by a witchdoctor. Yes, believe it, that still goes on.

Bizarrely, there were crows on the top of the aviary looking for a way in. They'd presumably spotted the free lunches being handed out. A few animals, young antelopes mostly and warthogs, were out on parole, grazing on the grass, snuffling in the dirt, or simply soaking up the sun.

We finally arrived at Stoffels' enclosure. It was empty.

"Over here, please try to keep up."

Stoffels looked as nonchalant as honey badgers always do, even when they're tackling a python, or a couple of lions. Following one of his escapes, Stoffels headed for the lion enclosure and got into a bit of bother. It must have been like a kindergarten kid punching Mike Tyson's knees. He spent two months in the infirmary and then escaped from that, heading straight back to the lions to get his revenge but he was fortunately intercepted by a keeper.

Places like Moholoholo perform an important role in raising public awareness about issues affecting wildlife, not least the importance of keeping a lid on poaching. It's an ancient activity, rarely driven by need these days, nearly always by greed, and will never be totally wiped out. Moholoholoians refer to the animals that can't be returned to the wild as ambassadors for their species; a vulture with a broken wing that hasn't mended properly, orphaned animals like Stoffels who were reared by people and simply won't cope if they're dumped back in the bush. Just being where they are tells a compelling story.

Stoffels isn't the only escape artist to make the news. Virtually all wild animals are confined to game reserves in Southern Africa, albeit some the size of small countries. But fences are more of a suggestion than a prohibition to some species, notably leopards, baboons, and warthogs. The former routinely go up and over the top, warthogs tunnel underneath. They go back the same way, not a problem, at least as far as they're concerned.

Elephants simply charge and flatten an electric fence if there's real motivation to get to the other side—fruiting marula trees being a prime example. The small shocks they might get are a momentary annoyance, and that's assuming the power is flowing. Given continual maintenance issues and the poor state of the national grid, that's not always so.

Lions tend to be opportunists, taking advantage of any hole in the fence, including holes made by poachers, or a gate inadvertently left open.

When elephants and lions do get loose, it naturally causes a stir; social media lights up and the radio gives regular updates on sightings. Lions can quickly cover a lot of ground when they decide to go exploring, but when they get into a populated area, everyone knows about it, including the rangers looking for them, thanks to the ubiquity of mobile phones. They're darted with a tranquilizer, lifted onto the bed of a small truck and taken back home.

Finding an elephant that's broken out usually isn't an issue either. They tend to stand out in a crowd, of course, and they usually have a specific gastronomic reason for going AWOL, so it's not too difficult to figure out where they're headed. Or so I'm told. Every now and again they break out onto the R40, the main north-south road traversing our area, to get at the marula trees fruiting there. Darting them isn't a first option because you need a crane to lift a sleeping elephant, and a very large truck to move it. All that takes time and motorists start to get impatient; a cacophony of blaring horns isn't going to help. The responsibility for sorting out the rodeo falls on rangers from the elephants' home reserve, but rangers from neighboring reserves pitch in when needed. So do the police and Farm Watch, a highly regarded local security company that works in close cooperation with area police and wildlife services. With all that goodwill and expertise, virtually all elephant excursions have a happy ending.

A community willing to pitch in, devote time and resources, including light aircraft and helicopters when needed, explains why wildlife estates around Hoedspruit have been so successful in combating poaching, and, as a by-product, crime in general. Visitors often tell us that we must feel safe from thieves and cutthroats, surrounded as we are by dangerous wild animals. Yes, that's true, but the animals need protecting too, it's that kind of vicious wider world. We're in a raft on a troubled sea, kept afloat by the passion and dedication of a small band of brave men and women.

riders on the storm

The technician tasked with linking us to the internet when we first moved into the cottage had a difficult time trying to get a steady signal. Up on the roof, he turned the dish this way and that, moved it as high as it could go on its pole, and then climbed down, had a cup of coffee, and disappeared for about two weeks.

In the interval we had no phone, TV, or internet connection. It felt as though the world was quickly moving on without us, which was vaguely concerning. How would it manage, lacking our daily input and expertise? We were fine; it was good to settle back into the 1970s for a while, apart from the risk of overdosing on Scrabble in the evenings.

Marie's Singer sewing machine was dusted off and she eagerly began mending hems on frocks and tears in shirts and skirts. Before that could happen, she had to find the right needles. The Singer had belonged to her granny and dated back to the 1950s, maybe even before that; it seemed very unlikely a dot on the map like Hoedspruit would have a shop stocking the needles for such a fossil.

An internet search was out of the question, but friends and acquaintances were still available. Many referrals and suggestions later, Marie found a man running a backyard business that specialised in fixing fridges, washing machines, and other large appliances. It was a long shot, but it turned out he was also proficient at finding needles in haystacks or, more accurately, in a rusted tin on a high dusty shelf at the back of his shed.

"I haven't sold one of these since, well, ever," the owner said, handing over a small, yellowed paper packet full of exactly the right needles.

Marie reverentially held the little packet in the palm of her hand. The still gleaming needles had an amazing story to tell involving a journey that began long ago in a factory in Glasgow, Scotland. Fate took them over the storm-tossed sea to a fabled far away land filled with wild beasts, where they finally found succour in a biscuit tin and were forgotten for about eighty years. Aladdin's lamp held fewer mysteries than that rusted tin.

"How much?" I asked.

The owner looked startled by the question. If you've just opened the Ark of the Covenant and taken out a small packet, that's not the question you expect to be asked. He shook his head slowly from side to side.

"No charge," he replied.

Marie doesn't normally hug strangers, and she didn't hug him, but we were both moved by his generosity. That kind of thing doesn't only happen in small towns and villages, but it's rare to non-existent in big cities. It was another reminder that little places usually have big hearts; people need each other and they're happy to help each other, to go the extra mile.

During this happy interlude, we were also astonished to discover that Hoedspruit had a public library, albeit a tiny one, clinging on for dear life at the edge of the municipal compound. An enormous librarian sitting on a typist's stool at a worn and chipped old desk took up a quarter of the space, partly blocking the entrance. I marveled at that little stool, the sheer engineering brilliance that enabled it to maintain its structural integrity under such a colossal load. I wormed my way in and bent down to look at a book on a low shelf. My extended backside inadvertently shunted a fellow bibliophile into the reference section. I apologized of course, but she was too busy trying to stabilize the wobbling encyclopedias and dictionaries to notice. It was that tiny.

Without TV or phones, those few days were tranquil days indeed. The sun shone, not too hot, and breezes came when they felt like it and played with the leaves on the trees. Impalas and nyalas came by every day with dainty nervous steps, standing and staring as if asking for permission to drink from our small pond. After a lifetime, I'm still amazed at the astonishing beauty and grace of impalas, their dark liquid eyes and gentle painted faces, and especially by their endearing politeness and good manners. All animals were obviously created by an artist with infinite talent and infinite time to spare, but impalas are my favorites.

Late one afternoon, the technician came back. He brought a helper with him and a very long pole. They went up on the roof and within an hour, we had a solid connection. That evening, I turned on the TV and the world barged back in to show off all its wars and share its squabbling voices. Watching and listening to the news, at least for me, is increasingly like having a dust devil form and start spinning in my head, raising detritus, building stress, devouring the sensible in a pointless, opaque, and directionless maelstrom. A moment that will be forgotten in a day, a week, a month, or a year achieves an importance so incandescent and consuming that people lose their reason.

Stress isn't just a human problem of course, never has been. In the 1970s, African antelope at a safari park in England's green and pleasant land were dying of heart disease at an excessive rate and vets scratched their heads trying to figure out why. They eventually decided that boredom was the cause, and the solution was to move them to a paddock next to a pride of lions. This kept the antelope constantly on edge and that apparently did wonders for their cardiovascular systems, or so it was claimed. Apparently, nothing keeps you on your toes better than large carnivores eyeing you and licking their lips.

I don't know how the story ended, but I suspect the antelopes eventually began to die of fright.

We're frequently told that constant stress in humans is a major cause of heart disease. But slouching around and doing nothing all day is also a bad idea, especially according to my big sister, Suzanne. She gathered up my dinky toys from the couch when I was nine and chucked them in the dustbin.

"Get off the couch and grow up," she demanded.

Just thought I'd get that off my chest.

But which is it?

I decided to ask the doctor at my next six-monthly check-up.

"You're seventy-six, the lions haven't eaten you yet, don't worry about it," she said, tearing a sheet from her prescription pad.

What was that "yet" about?

"And don't spend too much time on the couch," she added as I left.

Women and couches, riddles wrapped in enigmas.

To be fair, I think she was probably a bit stressed and distracted herself. The waiting room was full of people impatiently flicking through magazines, eager for their turn to debate a new medical theory being expounded by a self-proclaimed expert on the internet. The internet is a great place to find out about the five foods that are eager to sign your death warrant/allow you to live forever. All you have to do is like, subscribe, and ring the bell.

I suppose the real answer lies in finding the right balance in life, never an easy task. In the old days, my teenage days, hip people with rucksacks headed for the Himalayas in their sandaled thousands. They were seeking a skinny person standing in the snow on one leg, dressed only in a loin cloth, hands pressed together, with a beatific look on his face. He'd have the answer. But I suspect he froze to death long ago or maybe moved to

California and bought some proper threads.

As I mentioned at the start of this book, we moved here mainly because Michael and his family moved to Hoedspruit. They moved, at least in part, to escape the rat race. That's a phrase much used by the disenchanted. The original racing rats were competing to find a piece of cheese hidden at the center of a maze set up by psychologists with nothing better to do. I don't know what the purpose of that experiment was, but it seems cruel and pointless, like many corporate jobs. But at least you now know, if you didn't know before, why the boss is called "the big cheese," or, if the boss is female, "the big Gorgonzola."

Being small, intimately connected to nature, and, as importantly, distanced from the whirring cogs of the modern societal machine, Hoedspruit can provide solace for tired hearts and minds. It's an environment that enables people to discover or rediscover the best in themselves and then more easily find the good in others. It's not the Utopia that many Hoedies choose to believe, though belief is something nobody can truly do without.

Will the Hoedies' Utopia last? No, not forever, nothing does. But that's not the point. It exists in the here and now, and that should be enough.

My old bones are four years older than they were when we came slowly down the Abel Erasmus Pass, driving behind that monstrous truck full of toilet paper and sundries. It's been a great adventure, one I never expected to have at this stage of my life, but I'm near the last word in this book, nearer to the end of my own story. The full stop that's been hurtling towards me from the day I was born is getting closer by the second. This could be it.

author's postscript

Old people are often on first name terms with their local pharmacists, which is not surprising, given the number of visits they make. Our pharmacist's name is John. I'd been told John was Malawian, so when I first met him, I asked if he missed Malawi. He was visibly offended.

"I'm Ghanaian," he said emphatically.

I was briefly puzzled by his indignation but soon remembered that Malawians living hereabouts aren't usually highly educated, trained professionals. They generally work as gardeners, waiters, or in domestic service, if they can find work at all. Some are in the country illegally. As far as I know, John has nothing against Malawians, but he clearly didn't want to be lumped in with the local stereotype. Getting to know him, it turned out he lives in one of the eco-estates and his children attend the same school as our granddaughter, Jemima.

Whatever their individual place on the spectrum of reflected light, the people you see in Hoedspruit—waiting on tables, fixing cars, laying bricks, treating patients, running businesses, retired, or just passing through—could have come from anywhere. Tourists are all passing through of course, and they outnumber the locals at times, or so it seems.

In this respect, Hoedspruit is unlike other small towns in South Africa, many of which now have dense suburbs consisting of low-cost social housing with a much bigger footprint than the original towns themselves. Penned in by wildlife estates and game reserves, and to a lesser extent by commercial farms, there's little room left in Hoedspruit for urban sprawl. There is a small informal settlement close to the main commercial area but most people who work in town or in one of the surrounding wildlife estates commute from Acornhoek, a much larger town about eighteen miles to the south.

Given this reality, the wildlife estates around Hoedspruit are sometimes held up as examples of "green apartheid" because most, but by no means all, of the people who live in them are white. That's a result of individual inclination, means, and choice, not prejudice. Although many middle class black South Africans can well afford to buy property in eco-estates, few do so. But the town nevertheless features in a broader national debate in South Africa about environment, community, and the pursuit of a just society.

The frustration felt by those with high ideals can be a powerful motivator for change. People who are most disappointed with the current state of the world as they perceive it often become activists and leaders, driven by emotional pain to improve conditions for themselves and others. This has always been a constant aspect of human life. But proponents of a perfect world are always disappointed. Many philosophical and psychological schools of thought suggest that challenge, struggle, and imperfection are essential components of a meaningful human experience. Without these contrasts, concepts like happiness, success, and purpose would lose their value. The pursuit of a perfect world might inadvertently remove the very things that give life meaning.

Hoedspruit's embrace of conservation and sustainability embodies a powerful form of idealism, yet it is precisely this pursuit of perfection that can give rise to feelings of alienation in others. Eco-estates and private reserves offer near pristine landscapes and secure living for a few people and wild animals, but their necessarily limited capacity often means that access is confined to those with significant financial means. The drive to create a "perfect" green community can inadvertently reproduce patterns of segregation reminiscent of the past, underscoring the tension between environmental ideals and social realities.

Watching antelope grazing in the twilight bush, unaware of the leopard stalking them through the long grass, I sometimes think of Eden, the timeless allegory handed down by calloused hands from the dawn of human civilisation. Eden was a perfect world, but not, it seems, a world our ancestors were ultimately content to live in.

Tempus ostender. Time will tell.

www.ingramcontent.com/pod-product-compliance
Lightning Source LLC
LaVergne TN
LVHW020847180926
848329LV00027B/297

* 9 7 8 1 9 6 0 8 0 3 6 0 3 *